Never has there been su~~~ a ne~~~ ~~~ ~~~ ~~~ necessary time, for the body of Ch~~~ When It~~~ ~~~ part gives you a behind-the-scenes look at how to survive a life-altering crisis. It is transparent enough to show you all the deep pain of betrayal and brokenness but yet transforming enough to inspire you to live again. In this book you will find the strength to last through the night, for joy cometh in the morning.

—PASTOR ISAAC PITRE
CHRIST NATIONS CHURCH
TEXARKANA, TEXAS

Many people can quote scriptures about how to face trials. But Riva Tims has walked through the valley of pain and lived to tell about it. She has walked through the fire…but she's not bitter, sarcastic, or discouraged. She's learned how to hold on to God when your world falls apart. I know her story will restore hope to many who are ready to give up.

—J. LEE GRADY
CONTRIBUTING EDITOR, *CHARISMA* MAGAZINE
AUTHOR, *10 LIES THE CHURCH TELLS WOMEN*

As Christian leaders we are not automatically immune to pain during trials and tests of our faith. *When It All Falls Apart* is an inspiring pastoral tool that can build hope in the midst of hopelessness, especially in the lives of believers who may be preconditioned through religiosity to habitually rush to numb our pain. Instead, Pastor Riva Tims's story encourages us to learn to listen for the spiritual truths of what the pain that God allows is trying to teach us. Her transparency is courageously honest, truthful, and insightful. Reading this book will bless your soul.

—PASTORS R. DOUGLAS & ROSLYN CHUKWUEMEKA
NEW DESTINY CHRISTIAN CHURCH
LAVEEN, ARIZONA

It takes courage to draw strength from pain and devastating loss. *When It All Falls Apart* is a testimony and instruction manual for dealing with difficult challenge. It offers insight concerning how to move toward restoration and victorious promise. In this book Pastor Riva gives practical and pragmatic counsel from her personal experience of making sense of life's broken pieces and on the journey, through God, of putting life back together again. We love her advice, wisdom, sense of humor, common sense, warmth, and sincerity.

—BISHOP LYLE DUKES AND PASTOR DEBORAH DUKES
HARVEST LIFE CHANGERS
WOODBRIDGE, VIRGINIA

WHEN IT
ALL
FALLS
APART

WHEN IT ALL FALLS APART

RIVA TIMS

CHARISMA
HOUSE

Most CHARISMA HOUSE BOOK GROUP products are available at special quantity discounts for bulk purchase for sales promotions, premiums, fund-raising, and educational needs. For details, write Charisma House Book Group, 600 Rinehart Road, Lake Mary, Florida 32746, or telephone (407) 333-0600.

WHEN IT ALL FALLS APART by Riva Tims
Published by Charisma House
Charisma Media/Charisma House Book Group
600 Rinehart Road
Lake Mary, Florida 32746
www.charismahouse.com

Unless otherwise noted, all Scripture quotations are from the Holy Bible, New International Version. Copyright © 1973, 1978, 1984, International Bible Society. Used by permission.

Scripture quotations marked ESV are from the Holy Bible, English Standard Version. Copyright © 2001 by Crossway Bibles, a division of Good News Publishers. Used by permission.

Scripture quotations marked ISV are from the International Standard Version of the Bible. Copyright © 1996-2008 by The ISV Foundation. All rights reserved internationally. Used by permission.

Scripture quotations marked KJV are from the King James Version of the Bible.

Scripture quotations marked NAS are from the New American Standard Bible. Copyright © 1960, 1962, 1963, 1968, 1971, 1972, 1973, 1975, 1977, 1995 by the Lockman Foundation. Used by permission. (www.Lockman.org)

Scripture quotations marked NKJV are from the New King James Version of the Bible. Copyright © 1979, 1980, 1982 by Thomas Nelson, Inc., publishers. Used by permission.

Scripture quotations marked NLT are from the Holy Bible, New Living Translation, copyright © 1996, 2004, 2007. Used by permission of Tyndale House Publishers, Inc., Wheaton, IL 60189. All rights reserved.

Cover design by Justin Evans
Design Director: Bill Johnson

Library of Congress Cataloging-in-Publication Data

Tims, Riva.
When it all falls apart / Riva Tims. -- First edition.
pages cm
Includes bibliographical references.
ISBN 978-1-61638-471-5 (trade paper) -- ISBN 978-1-61638-634-4 (e-book)
1. Consolation. 2. Healing--Religious aspects--Christianity. 3. Bible--Quotations. 4. Tims, Riva. I. Title.
BV4905.3.T49 2012
248.8'6--dc23

2011048120

12 13 14 15 16 — 9 8 7 6 5
Printed in the United States of America

DEDICATION

To my children, Zoelle, Zachery III, Zahria, and Zion.
You are precious gifts from God. You have gone through much heartache and pain through no fault of your own. Yet each of you has
decided to stand in the grace and mercy of God. I admire your resil-
ience and determination to press past every obstacle and move forward
in your life and faith. You have a legacy in the Most High God, and
your latter will be greater than your former. I declare that you shall
walk in the fullness of your purpose and destiny.

CONTENTS

ACKNOWLEDGMENTS

There are many people without whose love, prayers, input, and support this book would not have been possible. To my parents, Fred and Rita Jennings—thank you for literally sacrificing your lives to assist me with the children. Your presence gave us a sense of stability when everything around us seemed to be shifting. Words cannot express how much I appreciate the love you have shown all of us.

To my twin sister, Rená Jones (aka "Boss Lady")—you take charge with a spirit of excellence. Thank you for being the best sister in the universe and an amazing church administrator. There is no way I could accomplish what I do without you.

Pastor R. Douglas and Roslyn Chukwuemeka, thank you for your continued love, support, and prayers. You have been an amazing spiritual covering for me and the members of Majestic Life Church.

Michele DeCaul and Varian Brandon, thank you for your intercession. You were my spiritual midwives. When I could barely lift my head, you helped me press through in prayer until I saw breakthrough.

To Majestic Life Church—you all are so special to me. Thank you for your love and your dedication to the Lord's work. I want to see you mature in Christ and maximize your gifts in Him so you can live the majestic life. God has an incredible plan for each of you and for our church.

I also thank the Lord for the many men and women of God who spoke into my life and gave me encouragement that aided in my healing process. I want to give special thanks to Bishop Lyle and Pastor Deborah Dukes, Pastor Randy Morrison, Pastor Isaac and Denisha Pitre, Paul McDonald,

Prophetess Jennifer McKesey, Prophetess Sheila J. Spencer, Bishop Andre and Jocelyn Williams, Pastor Rick and Fran Grant, Pastor David and Karen Jacques, Apostle Dannie and Precious Williams, Apostle VW and Erie Jones, Minister Karin Haysbert, Pastor Edith Young, Pastor Tanya Greene, and Pastor Timothy and Stafonda Lee.

Thank you for seeing the gifts God placed in me, even when I couldn't, and for continually reminding me that my season of breakthrough was coming. Your prayers, honesty, and wisdom helped me realize that God wasn't finished with me yet and that He had a purpose for the pain. I believe this book is part of that purpose. I love you all.

PREFACE

WHEN IT ALL Falls Apart was written after one of the most difficult seasons in my life. After a public scandal, I had lost my marriage, the church I helped found, and the life I had known for nearly fifteen years. There were times when I didn't think I would make it through the grief, which seemed unbearable, but I found that God is faithful.

Pain, anger, hopelessness, and confusion pushed me to search for books and materials that would help me. I didn't look for books with titles such as *Victorious Over the Enemy* or *More Than a Conqueror*. I wasn't able to identify with victory at my lowest point. I felt defeated. I was looking for titles that talked about being crushed like a bug. So when God brought me through my valley season, I wrote this book to give hope to the hopeless. I wanted readers to know there is something you can do when it all falls apart.

This book is the road map the Lord gave me to reach a place of healing and wholeness. Little did I know I would walk another painful journey. Several months after the manuscript was completed, my ex-husband, Pastor Zachery Tims, Jr., died suddenly at the age of forty-two. When he passed away, I found myself returning to the pages I had written for comfort.

When I began in ministry nearly twenty years ago, I had no idea what God would allow into my life. After enduring trials I once thought would kill me, I made a decision to help others who are chosen to walk through painful situations so they too can experience wholeness. I learned through my journey that true healing is possible, but it can be found in only one place—in Jesus Christ. He is the only one who can heal the anger, depression, and loneliness that follow tragedy and loss. He alone can mend a broken heart.

Healing is a process. It does not happen overnight. But because of God's incredible healing power, I was no longer mired in unforgiveness when my ex-husband died. That was possible only because I was willing to follow the leading of the Holy Spirit through the entire healing process. Too many people give up too soon. I pray this book motivates you to not give up, no matter how painful your trial. God will give you beauty for your ashes, the oil of gladness for mourning. God used my tests to make me stronger than I was before. I hope you will let Him do the same for you.

INTRODUCTION

As I stared in the mirror, I didn't recognize my own reflection. Stress and depression had taken a toll on my face and body. Barely able to stand, I could feel my heart beating rapidly, and my stomach was tied in knots. It had been several days since I had eaten. My face was gaunt and my eyes were sunken. I felt as though I had lost twenty pounds overnight.

The image in the mirror was also a reflection of my spirit man—weak and virtually void of life. I wasn't sure if God was hearing my prayers, and I began to question whether I would live through this pain.

The thought of leaving the earth appealed more to me than suffering through such agony. For weeks I had been crying out to God, asking Him, "Why?" I had been faithful in my Christian walk since I was a child. I couldn't understand how this could be happening to me. I rehearsed my life from childhood to the present, desperately trying to figure out what I had done wrong to deserve this type of suffering.

Perhaps you've been there. Perhaps you've asked God, "Why me?" Maybe you've wondered why you had to go through a painful experience or why bad things happen to good people. These are the kinds of questions that often follow traumatic events, such as the death of a loved one, divorce, financial collapse, or the diagnosis of a terminal illness.

Just like me, many in the body of Christ hold on to well-known scriptures that proclaim, "If ye be willing and obedient, ye shall eat the good of the land" (Isa. 1:19, KJV), or "Seek ye first the kingdom of God, and his righteousness; and all these things shall be added to you" (Matt. 6:33, KJV).

It's always a good idea to remind yourself of God's Word. But what do you do when you have been willing and obedient while seeking God's kingdom first, and yet tragedy still visits your life? Does that mean the Bible isn't true or that somehow God forgot about you? Absolutely not!

It took me awhile to come to that realization. I understand how Christians can become dismayed and bewildered when they go through traumatic circumstances. I felt the pressure that causes some people to lose hope and abandon the faith. But after walking through what I thought was the valley of the shadow of death, I am here to tell you that God hears you in those darkest hours, and He will answer.

The Bible tells us to "count it all joy when ye fall into divers temptations; knowing this, that the trying of your faith worketh patience. But let patience have her perfect work, that ye may be perfect and entire, wanting nothing" (James 1:2–4, KJV). When I was at my lowest point of depression, these scriptures gave me a renewed sense of hope and faith. They helped me realize that God never leaves us or forsakes us.

When tragedy strikes, we're faced with two decisions. We can either choose life, or we can choose death. Choosing death is easier, but I thank God that I chose to let my situation make me better not bitter. I thank God that He showed me how to triumph through my valley experience and come out bolder and more determined than ever to walk in my purpose.

My prayer is that this book will encourage you and show you that there is a divine purpose in your struggle and that you should never let your circumstances, no matter how severe they are, cause you to abort your destiny. Romans 8:18 says it well: "The sufferings of this present time are not worthy to be compared with the glory which shall be revealed in us" (KJV).

As you read my story, I am believing God that you will receive the revelation that this life is temporal. There is an eternity waiting for us, and "our light and momentary troubles are achieving for us an eternal glory that far outweighs them all" (2 Cor. 4:17). It may seem impossible to believe, but the trials we face will come to an end. What we do for Christ with this little time we have on earth is what will last.

So I invite you with me on this journey. Finding strength in the storm wasn't easy, and I don't sugarcoat the battle I faced. But God's grace truly is sufficient. When the world as I knew it fell apart, I made an incredible discovery: God was right there in the middle of the mess. He gathered the shattered pieces of my broken heart and made me brand-new. He's no respecter of persons. Just as He was with me in my darkest hour, He is there with you too.

CHAPTER

1

WHEN YOUR WORLD FALLS APART

I had just returned to my hotel room after preaching at a women's conference, still full in the Spirit from the powerful move of God that night. Before I could even get settled in my room, the Holy Spirit began to speak to me, His voice crystal clear. I listened intently as He began to tell me that something was wrong in my home. I did not fully understand what the Lord was revealing to me at that time, but I would soon find out.

Just a few days after the conference I learned that my husband, Zachery, had been unfaithful for some time. Because we were pastors of a thriving megachurch, word of his infidelity hit the gossip blogs and even became the subject of local and national news reports. I knew my husband wasn't perfect, but I never expected anything like this. The sin that was being brought to light made me question whether I ever really knew him.

Over the next several months as I learned of other affairs, I became physically ill, emotionally drained, and spiritually depleted. There were times when I literally thought I would die. My world was falling apart, and I felt there was nothing I could do but stand by helplessly.

You've probably heard the phrase "life happens." I mean, even the Bible tells us that we are all susceptible to difficult times. We read in Ecclesiastes 9:11 that "the race is not to the swift, nor the battle to the strong, neither yet bread to the wise, nor yet riches to men of understanding, nor yet favour to men of skill; but time and chance happeneth to them all" (KJV).

Ironically, though we know "life happens," we rarely expect life to happen to us in the way it so often does. Traumatic events can shake us to the very core of our beings. They can cause our sense of what's real to come crashing down, and they can replace our zeal for life with an overwhelming, overpowering heaviness that leaves us feeling numb.

Life happens to all of us. It happens when a marriage unravels under the strain of lies, infidelity, and deceit. It happens when an entire life savings is exhausted to offset a weak economy. It happens when the unexpected death of a loved one causes a paralyzing depression.

One thing you can be sure of is that life will happen. It will bring any number of events that usher in pain and feelings of hopelessness. The question is, how will you respond? Will you become bitter or better? Will your faith in God fail the test or pass with flying colors? Will you melt in the fire like plastic or become strong and refined like steel? These are the questions life will demand that you answer.

Life happened to Horatio G. Spafford and his wife, Anna. The couple enjoyed moderate fame in Chicago during the nineteenth century because of their successful law practice and close relationship with the evangelist D. L. Moody. But in 1871, the Great Chicago Fire ruined them financially when it destroyed most of the real estate they had amassed. Then in 1873, the ship on which Anna and their daughters were traveling to England sunk, killing all four of their girls.[1]

Devastated, Horatio Spafford left Chicago to join his grief-stricken wife in England. I can't imagine how he must have felt when the ship he was taking passed over the place where his daughters perished. I imagine it would have been unbearable. Yet that night in his cabin Spafford summoned the strength to pen the lyrics to one of the most famous hymns of all time.

When peace, like a river, attendeth my way,
When sorrows like sea billows roll;
Whatever my lot, Thou has taught me to say,
It is well, it is well, with my soul.[2]

Where did Spafford find that kind of faith in the midst of his grief? The lyrics of his song point to 2 Kings 4. In that chapter the Shunammite woman's only son suffered a heat stroke and died in her arms. This was a son she had waited a long time to conceive, a son the prophet Elisha had prophesied she would have. When her son died, she put him on his bed, closed the door, and set out to see the prophet. And when her husband stopped her to find out why she was going to see Elisha, all she said was, "It shall be well" (2 Kings 4:23, KJV). Then upon her arrival at Elisha's house, when the prophet's servant greeted her and essentially asked, "Is everything OK?" she responded by again saying, "It is well" (v. 26, KJV).

In the midst of such grief, where did Spafford and the Shunammite woman find the strength to declare, "It is well"? They both had just lost children, an unspeakable tragedy for any parent, yet they found a supernatural resolve. I believe each was able to speak from the Spirit, "It is well," because each drew from the well of the almighty God. Isaiah 12:2–3 says, "Behold, God is my salvation; I will trust, and not be afraid: for the LORD JEHOVAH is my strength and my song; he also is become my salvation. Therefore *with joy shall ye draw water out of the wells of salvation*" (KJV, emphasis added). Horatio Spafford and the Shunammite woman drew strength from their relationships with God. They knew He could be trusted no matter the circumstances.

The Bible promises that we will face tribulation in this life (Acts 14:22). Tribulation does not discriminate based on ethnicity, gender, or socio-economic status. The business owner, pastor, politician, professional athlete, soccer mom, and blue-collar worker are equally vulnerable to economic devastation, divorce, incurable illness, betrayal, infidelity, and demonic attacks. But as God asks in Jeremiah 32:27, is there anything too hard for the Lord? The answer, of course, is an emphatic *no*. Whether you are facing financial chaos, infidelity, a bad medical report, or the death of a loved one, God is able to heal and renew you with living water in the midst of your pain. God is able to happen to life.

WHEN YOU DON'T KNOW WHAT TO DO

As I dialed the international telephone number, my heart sank within my chest. What was I going to say? Why do I have to do this? How would she respond to me? Then I heard her voice as she said, "Hello?" I felt utterly nauseous. Softly I introduced myself as the wife of the man with whom she was having an affair.

Obviously taken by surprise, she again said, "*Hello?*" I wanted to ask a thousand questions, but I didn't get the chance. She began to tell me of *her* pain. She and my husband had been seeing each other for fourteen months, and she did not understand how he could have abruptly ended the affair when I confronted him. She honestly thought their relationship would continue even after I was made aware of it. Now that he had stopped communicating with her, she felt she had wasted more than a year of her life.

I listened to her sulk, thinking, "I've been his wife for over fourteen *years*. Am I supposed to have sympathy for you?" The woman was so infuriated that he stopped seeing her, she began contacting media outlets and even some members of our church via Facebook, unabashedly sharing the scandalous particulars of their encounters. I wanted her to stop for fear my children would learn of these nasty revelations. I could not bear to see them humiliated publicly.

I humbled myself and pleaded with the woman to stop for the sake of my children, and she seemed to be listening. Supernaturally, by the end of the conversation God had given me a heart of compassion for this woman, and I managed to share the gospel of Jesus Christ with her. I sincerely hoped the Holy Spirit would take the seed I planted and cause it to grow in the woman's life.

When I ended the conversation and hung up the phone, I could think only of how my life lay in ruins. Most of the people around us seemed to be focused on seeing my husband restored so the church would not hemorrhage. I loved the church too, and I knew the members had been hurt. But I needed healing myself before I could help anyone else. I felt it was only a matter of time before I reached my breaking point, and I didn't know where to turn.

God eventually took me to Genesis 16 and counseled me through the story of two women who were also in crisis. You may recall the story of Abraham and Sarah (known as Abram and Sarai before God changed their names). God promised Abraham that he would be a great nation. The only problem was that he and his wife, Sarah, were childless, and Sarah was beyond her childbearing years.

So Sarah attempted to help God bring His promise to pass. She decided to give Abraham her maid Hagar as his wife so she could bear him a son. But after Hagar conceived, she began to despise Sarah. She flaunted the fact that she was expecting and Sarah was not. I can't condone all of Sarah's actions in this situation, but for all that she and Hagar did wrong, there is much to learn from their example. They can teach us both what to do and what not to do in times of crisis.

CONFRONT THE SITUATION

As soon as Sarah saw Hagar flaunting her perceived superiority, Sarah confronted her husband about it, saying, "My wrong be upon thee: I have given my maid into thy bosom; and when she saw that she had conceived, I was despised in her eyes: the LORD judge between me and thee" (Gen. 16:5, KJV). Sarah did not let the problem worsen; rather, she took immediate action. She claimed responsibility for her decision to bring Hagar into her family and communicated to Abraham that she didn't appreciate Hagar's attitude toward her.

Like Sarah, we must face problems head-on. If you have an unction in your spirit that your spouse is cheating, *confront*. If contention and strife are manifesting in your ministry, *confront*. If your savings account is dwindling to nothing, step out in faith to do something different. *Confront* the situation. God will meet you there. We have a tendency to believe our circumstances will correct themselves. I have news for you: if you do nothing, the situation will only get worse.

By confronting the situation, Sarah did not allow Abraham to prioritize others above her. Nor did she allow others to drive a wedge between her and her husband. She took immediate action to put her house in order.

How often do we enable the dysfunctional behavior of our spouses, children, or close friends by not confronting them about it? How often do we stand silent as those around us place their recreation, careers, or ministries before their marriages, friendships, or families? Sarah stood strong. She told Abraham, "My wrong be upon thee" (Gen. 16:5, KJV). In other words, Sarah said, "It's your fault that this is happening. I presented Hagar to you to see God's promise come to pass in your life. Not being able to meet your need myself, I allowed you to find someone who could. And the very thing I did out of love for you is alienating me from you."

I know there are probably women across the globe who can relate to Sarah's frustration. You were there when your husband had nothing. You worked extra shifts so he could finish graduate school. You gave up a career to raise the children. You sacrificed, and now he seems to value his job more than his family. Remember Sarah. She went to Abraham and said, "Look, you've got to get this thing in order. It can't be this way."

Marriages do not simply fall apart without warning. When infidelity surfaces, there were usually signs along the way, whether subtle or dramatic. Unfortunately, many people in the kingdom of God choose to mask their problems or avoid them altogether. This is especially true of those in prominent positions within the body of Christ. The absolute worst thing you can do is to cover up your problems. Take immediate action before the issue gets too big for you to deal with it.

DO NOT OPERATE IN YOUR OWN STRENGTH

It was extremely hard for Sarah to believe she would conceive a child at her elderly age, so she took matters into her own hands. Let's be real. How many times have you tried to solve your own problem because you could not accept God's seemingly illogical answer to your prayer? Or how often have you thought God was taking too long? Just like Sarah, we make a mess of things when we try to bring God's promises to pass in our own timing and strength (and we end up begging God to fix our mistakes quickly!).

Usually when someone is betrayed in marriage, business, or even ministry, the natural response is to want revenge. Some of the people around me could not understand why I was not upset with the other women in my husband's life. They didn't understand that I was livid with Zach and not the other women because I was in covenant with him, not them. I wanted *him* to feel the intense pain I was experiencing. I wanted to retaliate against *him*—to slash his tires and burn all of his clothes.

The Holy Spirit, however, would not let me do those things. I heard Him say, "Hold your peace, and I will fight your battle." As difficult as it was, I retreated into a cocoon and allowed my dear intercessory prayer warriors to cover me. Some people labeled that was an act of weakness, but in point of fact it was an act of incredible strength. Meekness is power harnessed. It often requires more strength in God to be quiet than to speak, to be still than to react.

DO NOT WALK IN DENIAL

Sarah did not operate in denial. She examined her situation and laid everything out on the table. We need to do the same. We need to examine our situations and lay everything before the Lord. Sarah didn't sugarcoat the problem; she operated in the spirit of truth and acknowledged the conflict she created by trying to assist God. Truth is not always pleasant. In fact, the truth can be quite painful. David asked the Lord to search him to find anything that wasn't right (Ps. 139:23–24). I believe that is one of the hardest tasks—to look in the mirror and examine yourself and your culpability, especially when you are in severe emotional pain.

People have a natural propensity to blame others for their misfortune. It's often easier to point the finger at someone else than to accept personal responsibility for bad decisions we made or for overlooking the warning signs. How many people see the dysfunction in their marriage but act as if nothing is wrong? That's *denial*. Many people would rather live a lie than face the inevitable pain that accompanies the truth.

Some tragedies take us totally by surprise, and others are just waiting to happen. God is long-suffering; therefore He allows us time to get things in order. I distinctly remember prophets and prayer partners warning me of my husband's infidelity, and I went to him on several occasions to confront him, yet he denied the affairs. Those were opportunities God had given us to possibly save our marriage. He gives countless others the same chances. Denial, however, keeps us from taking advantage of those opportunities and possibly experience healing.

Denial is like a dam. Dams redirect the flow of water but cannot stop it. If the water pressure builds up, the dam will eventually burst. Denial is the same way. It redirects our focus, but it doesn't actually change the situation. This is why denial is dangerous, because when that pain builds up, it will eventually need to find some way to escape.

When a loved one dies unexpectedly, the grieving family members or friends must be allowed proper time to grieve. Likewise those who have experienced betrayal by a friend or spouse must give themselves the time needed to detoxify emotionally. If they don't, grief will slowly usurp their joy, leaving behind anger and hopelessness.

It was confirmed in July 2007 that my husband had been unfaithful for some time. We told only a few family members and some close friends. But in October others began speculating about it online because my husband's mistress began contacting the media.

During this time leaders we respected encouraged us to keep a united front. I tried to live life as normally as possible before people who had looked to us as an example, but behind the scenes I was in torment. For three months I walked in denial, as if everything would be OK if we just kept up the facade. That was possibly the worst thing we could have done. Pretending that we were united led to more dysfunction, more infidelity, and more pain.

The following November I was given an ultimatum to commit to stay in the marriage. I still had not seen the kinds of changes in my husband that would allow me to begin to trust him again. And I could no longer walk in denial. I offered to stay married but remain separated, and he didn't want that arrangement. By December he was back in the pulpit preaching, though very little had been resolved. The issues that led to his infidelity still hadn't been addressed. At that point I knew I had to face the truth of my situation—a painful road lay ahead.

BE ANGRY AND SIN NOT

In Genesis 16:6, Abraham gave Sarah permission to do with Hagar as she pleased, and the Bible says she "dealt harshly" with Hagar. That phrase literally means Sarah physically beat Hagar. Although I don't condone Sarah's decision to abuse Hagar, I do believe there are times when we need to get aggressive in the Spirit with those who are disrupting our destiny.

We in the body of Christ can be guilty of not allowing people to express healthy emotions. We tend to think a person is not walking in forgiveness if he or she gets angry. There exists an unfounded belief that if a Christian raises her voice or becomes visibly upset, her faith is somehow compromised. This is untrue. Psalm 7:11 says God is an honest judge, and He gets angry with the wicked every day. Surely God's anger with sin is well placed. It is proper, based on His justice.

The Bible is rife with examples of how God got angry with sin and the people who were committing it. In Genesis 19 God destroyed Sodom and Gomorrah when it had become decadently wicked. In Judges 16:23–30 God restored Samson's strength so he could destroy the Philistines' temple to the god Dagon. In Acts 5:1–10 Ananias and Sapphira died instantly after lying to the Holy Spirit and Peter about how much money they had earned in the sale of their goods.

God is infinitely righteous, yet He gets angry. Why should we conclude that it is always wrong for us to get angry? The Bible says Moses was meeker than anyone else on earth (Num. 12:3). Yet on several occasions he acted and spoke with profound anger, and that response was appropriate (Exod. 32:19).

Even Jesus, the sinless One, flashed anger. In Matthew 21, He angrily drove the moneychangers and those transacting business out of the temple by turning over their tables (vv. 12–13). Did Jesus sin? Matthew 5:22 says, "Anyone who is angry with his brother *without a cause* will be subject to punishment" (ISV, emphasis added). Is not indignation against sin a just cause? Righteous anger is not sinful.

There are several chilling examples of Christians who misdirect their righteous anger toward sin and end up sinning themselves. For instance, while referencing a well-known late-term abortion specialist, pro-life activist Randall Terry asked his audience to "pray that this family will either be converted to God or that calamity will strike him."[3]

In a later speech about a different abortion doctor, Terry publicly said, "I hope someday he is tried for crimes against humanity, and I hope he is executed. I make no bones about it, friends. It is a biblical part of Christianity that we pray for either the conversion or the judgment of the enemies of God."[4] There is a difference between having righteous indignation and being vindictive.

When Paul admonished us to be angry and sin not (Eph. 4:26), he was acknowledging that everyone would experience anger. However, the anger must be directed at the sin and not lead us to commit sinful acts. By sinning ourselves, we become hypocrites.

After I learned of my husband's infidelity, I went through a period of depression; then I experienced an overwhelming wave of anger. Well-meaning church leaders told me it was not good for me to be angry. But I couldn't help but think that if someone had harmed one of their family members, or if a man had done to one of their daughters what my husband did to me, they would have experienced some anger themselves.

It is not easy to explain, but at the time I felt I had been murdered. Murder is a premeditated act that puts a life to an end. I use that term because felt my husband knew the destruction he was causing. We came out of a church where our pastor also had an affair. My husband saw firsthand how our pastor's infidelity devastated his wife, their children, and the ministry. I felt my husband fully understood the heartache he was unleashing on me and the church. And I was angry. I was angry with Zach for being unfaithful. I was angry at his attempts to cover up his infidelity. I was angry at sin—and I had the right to be angry.

In hindsight, I wish the people around me had validated my anger instead of encouraging me to repress it. The more I suppressed my indignation toward sin, the more I was subconsciously telling myself that my husband's actions were not that bad and that I was overreacting. I heard a long list of reasons why my husband was unfaithful—because of things in his past or because our former pastor had done the same thing. Not once did I hear the simple truth that he made a choice to sin. God gave him a way of escape, but he chose not to take it.

The people I turned to for help were so busy trying to explain my husband's hurtful choices they failed to understand that it was normal for me to be angry. I was criticized when I expressed anger. I remember in my anger calling one of the women Zach was involved with a whore, and I was reprimanded for that. I was never given an opportunity to go through the proper stages of healing, so my anger began to consume me.

I unleashed some of my frustration on the people I turned to for help because I was not seeing any progress. I said many things in anger to them and about them because I was in so much pain. In retrospect, I am sure they took my insults and complaints personally. Now that I have more perspective on the situation, I sincerely pray that they understand that I was speaking out of deep hurt and pain. I love each of those individuals and harbor no malice toward them.

I believe if I had been encouraged to address my feelings of anger instead of being pressured to quickly reconcile with my husband, I would have been better able to deal with the deep wounds my husband's infidelity left in my heart. And I would have been that much closer to being healed.

In Matthew 12 Jesus's mother and brothers came to Him while He was addressing a crowd. He turned to them and said, "Who is My mother and who are My brothers?" (v. 48, NKJV). Then He pointed to the crowd and said, "Here are My mother and My brothers! For whoever does the will of My Father in heaven is My brother and sister and mother" (vv. 49–50, NKJV). This passage shows that there were times when even Jesus had to draw a line in the sand. He loved His family, but they were not more important to Him than fulfilling God's call on His life. There will be times when you too will have to distance yourself from relatives and dear friends in order to pursue what God has for you.

Joseph's brothers were dream-killers. Although being separated from his family and sold into slavery were devastating for Joseph, it worked to everyone's benefit in the end. God ultimately put Joseph in a position to save everyone, including his family, from starvation during a season of famine (Gen. 37–50).

They may be well meaning, but if your employees, friends, or family members are sapping the life out of you, it may be time to create some distance. Change is hard, but it is also necessary. During the transition in my marriage, I had to ask the hard questions and make some even harder decisions. Was I supposed to act as if nothing happened or take a stand for righteousness?

I believe that God, in His sovereign love, exposed my husband's infidelity so restoration and deliverance could take place. I desperately wanted my husband and my marriage. But if restoration and deliverance were not taking place, should I have just stayed for appearance's sake? You may be able to attest to the fact that many ministers' wives stay with unfaithful husbands for the sake of appearances. Should I have also lived a lie and been miserable so others could avoid having to deal with the reality that we weren't the perfect couple?

As you learn to deal strongly with the people around you, you must also learn to effectively deal with yourself. It is not easy to ask yourself hard questions and require honest answers, but that is what it takes to bring lasting change.

Generally it is hard to hear, recognize, and take responsibility for the fruit we are producing in our lives. But I assure you, God will give you the grace to change the things He shows you when you ask yourself the tough questions. You may be allowing fear of separation, others' disapproval, or uncertain outcomes to prevent you from making needed adjustments. However, when you make the necessary changes by faith, God will release His best based on His promise to never leave you nor forsake you (Heb. 13:5).

OBEY GOD'S INSTRUCTIONS

After Sarah beat Hagar, the younger woman fled from Sarah's presence, and the Angel of the Lord found her by a spring in the wilderness. The angel asked Hagar how she had gotten there and where she was going. Hagar replied that she had run away from Sarah after being harshly treated. But after hearing Hagar's story, the angel had simple instructions for her: go back (Gen. 16:7–9).

Hagar too felt as though her world had been turned on its head. It was not Hagar's idea to pursue Abraham; Sarah arranged for Hagar to bear a child for her husband. Then when Hagar conceived, Sarah became angry and beat her despite the fact that Hagar was pregnant, forcing her to run away into the wilderness. I can understand why, like many of us, Hagar might have thrown herself a pity party.

The whole mess was Sarah's brainchild. Yet the Angel of the Lord told Hagar, "Go back and get it right. You were wrong. You shouldn't have disrespected Sarah because she had not conceived. It was not necessary to flaunt yourself like that and treat Sarah badly. Get back in there and submit yourself to her authority."

How often do we find ourselves in a similar situation? Rather than submit to God's instruction, we rebel because of our pride. Proverbs 16:18 warns us that pride comes before a fall. Don't let your situation become worse due to pride. Remember, for every seed sown, a harvest *will* be reaped. Hagar chose to be obedient, and she returned and submitted to Sarah.

I finally accepted what God had shown me and stopped denying the problems in my home. I knew I would have to walk a difficult road; the issues in my marriage and ministry were not going to magically disappear. Then I had to ask the hard questions and begin making the tough decisions. God gave me specific instructions on how to walk out my journey. He told me to hold my tongue. He said, "I will fight your battle." That meant I could not defend myself against all the accusations levied against me. Nor could I take revenge against those who hurt me. He firmly told me to hold my peace. That also meant I could not run to my dad, a former Recon Marine, and ask him to set things straight, if you know what I mean. God clearly said, "Hold your peace."

I am so glad I humbled myself and did not let my pride get the best me. I am now reaping a wonderful harvest of love because I followed God's instructions. My God operates in love, and His desire is that we all come to Him and allow Him to fully restore us.

LISTEN FOR GOD'S VOICE

Sarah eventually gave birth to a son of her own, Isaac, and at that time she again ousted Hagar from the camp. This time it was not because Hagar disrespected Sarah but because Hagar's son, Ishmael, taunted Isaac. Just like before Sarah instructed Abraham to deal with Hagar and her son. As a result, Hagar and Ishmael ended up alone in the wilderness with very little provision. But the Angel of the Lord again met Hagar and encouraged her by telling her that Ishmael would be a "wild donkey of a man" whose offspring would be too numerous to count (Gen. 16:12).

It is awesome that in the midst of our mess, God will still give us an encouraging word. God does not care whose fault it was, what mistakes were made, or what regrettable things were said. When you heed His call, open your eyes to the things of God, humble yourself, and begin to earnestly submit to Him, He will move you toward your destiny. God loves us, is there for us, and wants us to get back on course.

When your world is falling apart, the best thing to have is a word from the Lord. Prayer is the vehicle to hearing God's voice. A word from the Lord gives hope to the hopeless and light in the midst of darkness. God says His sheep know His voice and a stranger they will not follow (John 10:27). The enemy wants to speak to you during your time of tribulation. He wants to discourage you and rob you of your faith. You must drown out the voice of the enemy by praying and praising your heavenly Father.

I remember receiving all kinds of advice from well-meaning people. There was only one problem: their advice clashed with what I was hearing in my spirit from the Lord. Although their intentions were good, they were using a cookie-cutter strategy. Everyone's situation is different, and some couples need more time than others. I needed *a lot* more time to heal and process what happened.

I was given three months to decide whether to stay in the marriage. That was not nearly enough time for me to sort through the distrust, anger, and pain I felt, especially since I continued to learn of other acts of deception. Each time I discovered something new during that three-month period, I felt like I was starting the healing process over again. That ultimatum made me feel like I was being asked to sweep everything under the rug, and I could not do that.

Only God knows your end from your beginning. You must trust the Lord even in your darkest hour. What God began to tell me in my darkest hour is that He would assist in the healing process, allow me to take the time I needed, and verify whether my spouse really loved me. I followed the Lord's instructions, and I know I am whole and restored today because I did. He mended my broken heart; He restored my joy.

KNOW THAT GOD SEES YOU

After her encounter with the angel, Hagar blessed the name of the Lord, calling Him "the God who sees me" (Gen. 16:13). In her solitude, in her shame, in her confusion, and in her sorrow, God saw Hagar. Later, as a memorial of Hagar's encounter with God, that spring was named "the well of a living One my Seer."[5]

You see, many times during my valley season I felt as though I was invisible, as if no one saw me. Yes, people were looking, but it seemed very few were able to see how much I was hurting. Very few saw the pain and torment I was going through in the night season when I pressed tear-stained cheeks against my pillow and wept all night long. Very few saw me suffocating under the pressure of that unbearable pain.

Why couldn't they see? Why couldn't they understand? Because it is difficult for people outside your situation to fully comprehend what you are going through. And even when you try to give them an inkling of the magnitude of your pain, they might not know how to minister to your need. Eventually you stop trying to explain your hurt and just learn to deal with it, and those around you begin to think you're doing OK.

Let me reiterate to you what Hagar realized: God sees you. In the popular movie *Avatar* the Na'vi greeted one another by saying, "I see you." They were expressing the fact that they saw one another beyond the outer shell and were peering into the inner being. The Bible says that man looks on the outward appearance, but God looks at the heart (1 Sam. 16:7). God sees you at your core. He sees you in your messed-up situation. He knows what you do in secret.

But He not only sees you, He also wants to bring you out of where you are to fulfill the calling He has placed on your life. He wants to take you to another level of faith. God doesn't want to see you fail. He sees you, and He wants you to be empowered by His promise that He will never leave or forsake you. He wants you to be able to declare, "It is well," even in the face of death.

Wherever you are right now, God says, "I see you, and I'll fix it if you will be obedient." Go back and submit to authority. Go back and ask for forgiveness. Go back and forgive those who hurt you. God says, "Trust Me. I'm going to give you a strategy to deliver you when your world falls apart."

CHAPTER
2

WHY
ME ?

Probably at no other time since the Great Depression have so many people been asking, "Why me?" The weak economy has caused millions of Americans to lose their jobs, their homes, and, in some cases, their life savings. And for many there is no end in sight.

The words "why me" are usually uttered out of desperation, without premeditation. They come automatically when we're in the midst of extraordinary pain, fear, or confusion. The word *why* means "for what cause, reason, or purpose." It asks the intention, justification, or motive for an act.[1] For what cause was a person raped? For what purpose did a loved one die young? What was the intent behind that earthquake? What justification can be given when tithing believers lose their entire savings? *Why.* The very word screams devastation, yells pain, and shouts, "Help me!"

Our powerlessness over death explains why such despair often accompanies the invocation of why. Although the physical death of a loved one is tragic and the grieving process can be excruciating, the death of good health, a marriage, or a comfortable lifestyle can be just as agonizing.

Grief wrought by spiritual death is strikingly similar to the pain we experience after the passing of a beloved relative or friend.

The question still remains: Why must we experience this type of pain at all? The Bible is clear: some divine manifestations arrive only by way of death. Without the shedding of blood, there is no remission of sin (Heb. 9:22). Had Christ not conquered death and risen from the grave, we would not have everlasting life. John 12:24 says, "Verily, verily, I say unto you, except a corn of wheat fall into the ground and die, it abideth alone: but if it die, it bringeth forth much fruit" (KJV).

As unthinkable as it may be, tragedy allows us to see another dimension of God. Does it mean that God causes our affliction? No! But He does allow it, just as He allowed tragedy to befall Job. If life as you knew it seems to be over, I encourage you to take heart. It may just be the beginning of something new God is doing in you.

Let's go a little deeper. In the Gospel of John, Lazarus fell ill and ultimately died. Jesus, moved by news of Lazarus's death, told His disciples, "Our friend Lazarus has fallen asleep; but I am going [back to Judea] to wake him up" (John 11:11). The disciples, misunderstanding Jesus's metaphor, questioned His plan to travel back to Judea for someone who was merely sleeping (v. 12). So Jesus made the situation plain to them and said, "Lazarus is dead. And I am glad for your sakes that I was not there, to the intent ye may believe" (vv. 14–15, KJV).

Jesus used the word *intent*, which is one of the terms used to define the word *why*. For what intent did Lazarus fall ill and die? It was *so that we may believe*. Jesus waited until Lazarus's body began to stink before He showed up so the disciples would believe. What is dead and stinking in your life? Are you facing a situation that seems impossible to solve? What circumstance makes you think God does not care? Could it be that God is allowing the trial in your life to foster in you a deeper belief in Him?

It had been two years since my husband's infidelity was exposed. We were still married but living as though we were divorced. Two years and nothing had been finalized. Two years and there were still undressed wounds and raw feelings of rejection and abandonment. I could not comprehend why my life had taken such a devastating turn. I felt as though I was drowning in a sea of sheer hopelessness. There seemed to be a dark, thick fog covering every movement I made. I could honestly feel demonic oppression aggressively hindering my prayer and worship.

I felt like my husband was tormenting me on purpose. I am almost certain that's not true, but when a person is in excruciating pain, his perception can be unbalanced. I sincerely felt like a beautiful, expensive porcelain vase that had been carelessly thrown to the floor and shattered in an attempt to destroy any semblance of its beauty and value. I often asked my husband, "Why don't you care? Why won't you help me? Why don't you love me?"

Why? It felt as though my life had ground to a halt. I had no job security, no income, and no understanding of how my situation had gotten so bad so quickly. I could not understand why God was not making the situation better. Instead He was forcing me to endure a legal battle when I already felt defeated. I could not help but wonder if God was mad at me. I wondered again and again, "Why me, God?" Thankfully the Lord didn't let me stay there. He began to show me powerful tools to conquer the "Why me" syndrome.

You see, asking "Why me?" automatically places a person in a defeated mind-set. It feeds feelings of rejection because the person asking why typically feels abandoned. Rejection leads to low self-esteem, which in turn makes us feel unworthy of God's best.

The Book of Esther tells us of a young woman who had every reason to ask, "Why me?" Esther had lost her parents and lived with a cousin named Mordecai. Because she was female and her family was not wealthy, Esther was literally at the bottom of the societal totem pole. However, Esther ended up in the palace as queen (Esther 2:17–18). And because of her position, God gave her an important assignment—to save the Jewish nation.

Esther knew that in order to save her people, she would have to go before the king. That might sound like a simple thing, but if Esther approached the king uninvited, he could have her put to death. King Xerxes hadn't summoned Esther in weeks. Yet instead of sulking and asking God why, Esther confronted her situation and ultimately determined, "If I perish, I perish" (Esther 4:16). In other words, "If I die in the process of saving my people, then I die." From what source did Esther find the resolve to make such a proclamation? How was she able to stare death in the face instead of falling prey to the "Why me" syndrome?

I believe the source of Esther's strength to conquer "Why me" is revealed in her journey to become queen of Persia and is mirrored in Paul's letter to the Philippians. Both passages of Scripture show us how to go through a death experience and still end up with an amazing life. In Philippians 3:10–11 Paul makes a powerful statement that we will examine at length. He said, "That I may know him, and the power of his resurrection, and the fellowship of his sufferings, being made conformable to his death; if by any means I might attain to the resurrection of the dead" (KJV). This verse, along with the process through which Esther ascended to royalty, shows us that we conquer death through the authority we gain from intimately knowing God.

THAT I MAY KNOW HIM

After King Xerxes banished Queen Vashti and announced that he would be looking for a new queen from among the eligible young virgins, Mordecai took Esther to the king's palace. One of the first people Esther met there was Hegai, the keeper of the women. Esther found favor with Hegai, and he gave her everything she needed for purification so she would be ready to go before the king.

The name *Hegai* means "my meditation."[2] In the same way Hegai gave Esther what she needed to prepare to meet the king, so does prayer give us everything we need to be satisfied and strengthened in God. When Paul said in Philippians 3:10, "I want to know Christ," he was saying he wanted an intimate relationship with God. The only way you can be intimate with God is by praying and seeking Him through His Word. I must have a relationship with God because if I don't know Him, then I can't trust Him. But when I know Him, I can hear His voice and follow His instructions.

As I stared at my ceiling, I kept wondering if this was a bad dream. I still couldn't fathom how all this could be happening. I had been married for fourteen years, given birth to four beautiful children, and cofounded a megachurch. Zach and I were supposed to be an example for our children and church members, but our current situation fell well short of that mark.

I kept getting stuck in memory lane. I continually rehearsed all the time I had invested in my marriage. Where had it landed me? I felt as though I had been thrown away like a piece of trash. I thank God for my family and a few close friends who never took sides but showed me and Zach unconditional love and support. I was so hurt, I wanted to hate my husband and everyone in my life who I felt let me down. But even when I couldn't see my way in the darkness, I could still hear the beautiful voice of God. Because I remained intimate with Him, God became my lifeline.

The Bible says that God "fulfills the desire of those who fear him; he hears their cry and saves them" (Ps. 145:19). His voice led me through the pitch-black darkness. When I was depressed, I could hear Him say, "All things will work together for the good to them that love Me and are called according to My purpose" and "I will never leave you nor forsake you." (See Romans 8:28; Hebrews 13:5.) Though I couldn't feel God, I could still hear God because I knew His voice. Knowing God intimately is the key to unlocking the hidden triumph in the trial.

THE POWER OF HIS RESURRECTION

When we scream, "Why me?", we often don't realize that we are in the process of dying to the old so God can resurrect us with greater power, anointing, and faith in the new. Esther entered the palace as Hadassah, an orphan raised by her cousin. But she eventually became Queen Esther. How did Hadassah become the queen of Persia? The process was long and arduous.

In order for Hadassah to become Queen Esther, she was left in the care of Hegai to go through twelve months of purification. Purification is a process of focused and deliberate elimination of uncleanliness. Why did Esther have to endure that process for twelve months? To understand that, we must look at the Hebrew words for *twelve* and *months*.

The word translated "twelve" comes from the Hebrew term *shenayim*, which means to alter or given to change.[3] Esther was given twelve months to be transformed from an orphan girl into a queen. God wanted to bring a transformation in Esther's life that required more than a one-time stop at the altar. She couldn't be an overnight sensation.

Many of us want immediate results. We go to one service, pray one time, give one offering, and expect some significant breakthrough. But we must walk out this process daily, and we will go through various seasons before God's purpose manifests.

In order to be purified for God's purpose, we must commit to a process. The more you are in the Word, the deeper your understanding of God will become. The closer you get to the Son, the more imperfections you will see within yourself, and the more you will be challenged to make some adjustments. My old way of thinking began to change as I soaked in the Word of God. I realized that I didn't know as much as I thought I did. God caused me to dig into His Word and make sure what I had come to believe was actually true. As He renewed my mind, God was making me into a new creation.

The word for "months" in Esther 2 is translated from the Hebrew root *chodesh*, which means to be new or to rebuild.[4] The change this word refers to is like the transformation of a caterpillar into a butterfly. Caterpillars don't just grow wings and start flying. They *become* butterflies. They undergo a process through which the caterpillar develops into a new creature altogether.

During the first six months of Esther's preparation to become queen, she soaked with oil of myrrh (Esther 2:12). Myrrh is one of the ingredients in the holy incense used in the tabernacle, but it was also used for embalming the dead. To become beautiful in God's sight, we too must be purified so that Christ's character replaces our old, fleshly nature. It is painful to change when you've been a certain way for so long. It is bitter to endure spiritual surgery and allow the Holy Spirit to excise pride, self-reliance, and anything else hindering our relationship with God. But it is through the purification process that we become new.

My ob-gyn looked at me and wanted to know why I had come to see her. I could feel my heart pounding in my chest. What do I say? How do I say it? I couldn't open my mouth to speak. I had not thought far enough ahead when I made the appointment. Minutes went by as my eyes filled with tears. I purposed in my heart that I would not cry, not now. She again asked me why I made the appointment. I opened my mouth to speak with confidence and strength, yet my voice was fragile, soft, and still on the verge of breaking.

I said, "I need to be checked for STDs." I was utterly humiliated. I proceeded to explain that my husband had been unfaithful, but she was not interested in hearing the explanation. She looked at me as if to say, "I see this all the time. You pastors are no different from anyone else." *Ugh!* Tears rolled uncontrollably down my face.

I lost thirty pounds in two months from not eating properly. The stress of losing the life I had come to know caused my health to decline. Each new facet I learned about the years of deception crushed my spirit a little more. Pain pierced my chest day and night, and I often found myself rushing to the emergency room for medical assistance.

Unable to sleep I often drove around all night purposely trying to get lost. If it were not for my children, I probably would not have returned home. I kept wondering if my husband even cared. Did he ever love me? This made it virtually impossible for me to heal. My focus was on the wrong person. I was still looking to a man to provide physical and emotional support when God should have been my focus. Though I could not see it myself, I was in the process of being rebuilt into a stronger, wiser, better creation. God was getting rid of the impurities in my heart.

During the second six months of Esther's purification process, she soaked with sweet odors. One of the common ingredients in this mixture was calamus. Ancient Hebrew priests used to sprinkle calamus on the altar to counteract the odor of the blood left by the animal sacrifices. In a similar way, six months of soaking with sweet scents also got rid of the unpleasant odors that permeated the pores of the concubines.

I have learned that some people are delivered of certain sins and behaviors, but they still carry the residue. Gang members who get saved may no longer engage in ungodly activities, but people who meet them may still think they live gang lifestyles simply because of their clothes, speech, or mannerisms. The more time a person spends in a particular activity or lifestyle, the longer it will take for the residue of that behavior to fade.

But it does fade. The sweet scents Esther received during her purification process often took the form of a beautifying paste, which was rubbed all over the body to lighten a woman's skin and remove spots and blemishes. Likewise, when Christ purifies us, He removes our imperfections.

Often when people who have walked with Christ for long periods of time share their testimonies, it is hard to believe how they used to be. The transformation is so unbelievable because the residue from their past life is virtually impossible to see. They have truly become new creations. This is what God wants to do in everyone who calls on Him. The Bible says, "Therefore if any man be in Christ, he is a new creature: old things are passed away; behold, all things are become new" (2 Cor. 5:17, KJV).

The second six months of the preparation period also enabled the eunuchs to ensure the concubines weren't pregnant with a child who didn't belong to the king. The reason for this precaution may have been to protect the king from leaving an unrelated heir to his throne. Our purification process too allows us to see what seeds may be growing within us.

Seeds of bitterness, hurt, and betrayal can take root and lie dormant until we are put in a situation that causes them to germinate. The seed of rejection had been planted in my life years ago, but I chose to cover it instead of uprooting it. When my marriage was dying, those seeds began to mature and were trying to bear fruit.

God allows the fruit of these unhealthy and ungodly seeds to come to the fore so we can remove them and prepare for the next level in God's plan for our lives. God sees the end before the beginning (Isa. 46:10), and He knows exactly what is in our hearts (Ps. 44:21). He wants to make sure there are no impurities in our hearts that would hinder us from fulfilling His will.

There were so many times when I felt I would not make it through the day. It took faith just to breathe. As more and more evidence surfaced about the years of deception, I secretly wanted God to take me home to be with Him. I had convinced myself that I was totally justified in feeling like a victim. I never cheated on my spouse. I wasn't living a secret life of sin. I had practiced what I preached. Everything I was going through was my husband's fault.

When a dear friend asked me, "What is your responsibility in this?" I proudly responded, "I have none!" But my friend proceeded to show me that my error wasn't in what I did but in what I *didn't* do. I had been an enabler who allowed dysfunctional behavior to continue far too long. We will take a closer look at this in chapter 5.

The truth was extremely painful to hear. But God allowed me to soak in sweet odors, and the seeds of pride and self-righteousness and the root of bitterness that were lying dormant in me began to manifest. God did not want those seeds to bear fruit later in my journey. So He allowed a painful purging to take place to remove every seed and vanquish any residual odor of generational curses that permeated my family's bloodline.

The closer I got to the Lord, the more my imperfections were magnified. I became broken and contrite. As I allowed God to perform the delicate surgery to remove unforgiveness, hate, bitterness, pain, and torment, the ashes of death that wanted to overtake my life were exchanged for His beauty. The dark blemishes of pain were being erased, and my tear-stained face was beginning to glow even while I was still in the process of healing.

THE FELLOWSHIP OF HIS SUFFERING

No matter how many times I read it, I am always struck by Paul's words in Philippians 3:10: "Lord, I want to know You and the power of Your resurrection *and the fellowship of Your suffering*, becoming like You in

Your death." Why would Paul want to fellowship with Christ's suffering? And why would Paul arrange his prayer in that order?

Most of us don't want to suffer. We want to avoid pain, but trials are a part of life, and God uses them for our good. How? Our dependence on God increases when we enter difficult seasons or are faced with tragedy. And the closer we get to God, the more we allow our old nature to die and God to resurrect us as new creations. When we are rebuilt, we are able to face the enemy with *dunamis*, God's miracle-working power.[5] When we endure trials, we gain a power that is much more potent than it was before our death experience.

This process reminds me of *The Six Million Dollar Man*, a 1970s television series in which an astronaut named Steve Austin is severely injured in a horrible crash and loses his legs, one arm, and an eye. He is rebuilt with bionic replacements for his legs, arm, and eye at a cost of $6 million, and the new body parts give him superhuman strength. *The Bionic Woman* was a spin-off of the show. The main character, Jaime Sommers, was a professional tennis player who was nearly killed in a skydiving accident. She too was surgically rebuilt with bionic implants that amplified her hearing, strengthened her right arm, and enabled her to run faster than a speeding car.

In the same way Steve Austin and Jaime Sommers were rebuilt after a tragedy almost killed them, so too can we be remade through trials. God allows each of us to experience the death of certain emotions and relationships so He can rebuild us and make us even better.

During my death experience, God rebuilt me and made me stronger. I am not the same. When my mind was in disarray, God gave me the mind of Christ. When I couldn't hear the Lord's voice, God gave me supernatural ears to hear that soft, sweet voice over the din of life. When I couldn't see through the darkness of deception and despair, God gave me supernatural vision to see the truth, no matter how painful. So now when I go through the valley, I have more anointing and experience to handle it. And I am better able to help someone else.

That is the fabulous part of this entire revelation. God strengthens us in the area where we were broken and damaged. We become stronger and more anointed to help someone else. So if you were broken in your marriage, health, finances, or emotions, those are the very areas God will strengthen so it will be harder for you to break when you face a new trial.

If you have ever broken a bone, you know that simple fractures usually take about six to eight weeks to heal, though it takes longer for larger or more fragile bones to heal. When a bone breaks, blood vessels rupture and cause a hematoma (blood-filled swelling) at the fracture site. A callus lump made of fibrous tissue and calcium forms in place of the hematoma. It holds the broken bone in place for the permanent repair. The callus becomes bonier as the cartilage is replaced by spongy bone. This bony callus remodels depending on the stress placed on it, and it becomes a strong, permanent patch at the fracture site. This part of the process can take as long as a year, but the bone is often stronger after the break than it was before.[6]

Just as a broken bone can mend itself and become stronger in the area that was originally broken, so can a couple's relationship become stronger after an affair, paving the way for them to help others in similar situations. God's ultimate desire is reconciliation for broken relationships, especially marriages. So too can broken finances, ministries, or trust actually become stronger after healing takes place.

There are some people who would never have started their own businesses had they not lost their jobs. There are people who never would have moved to their promised land if they hadn't been forced out of their homes. I am stronger today than ever. I am wiser, and I am walking in more faith because I believe God on a much deeper level.

WALK BY FAITH AND NOT SIGHT

Before he went on a national search for a wife, King Xerxes was married to Queen Vashti. She was a very beautiful woman who knew the dignity and privacy of royalty. Vashti knew that if the king had been sober, he never would have asked his queen to expose herself at his party. By disobeying the king, she refused to lower her standards. Yet because she would not be put on display in such a degrading manner, her crown was taken away, and the king divorced her on the spot.

Many times God works through unbelievers to fulfill His plan and promises. I don't know whether Vashti's actions were fueled by rebellion or dignity. What I do know is that Vashti had to get out of the palace so Esther could become queen. God is getting your palace ready too. You may be living in a one-bedroom apartment, but God is preparing to give you keys to your own home. You may be working forty to fifty hours a week and barely making ends meet, but God has already hand-picked the job or business opportunity that will transfer wealth into your hands.

My situation seemed impossible. I had been in ministry for over twelve years. My children, home, and church consumed my life. I really did not have anything of my own. I had recently sold my hair salon. I had not completed my master's degree in hospital administration. I didn't know who would want me if I ever desired to remarry; after all, I have four children, including one with special needs. I felt like Angela Bassett's character in the movie *Waiting to Exhale*. I supported my husband when he had nothing. I gave him my best years, or so I thought, and he just traded me out for someone else. I felt rejected and completely lost.

But the stone the builders rejected became my chief cornerstone (Ps. 118:22; Mark 12:10). In my rejected state I learned to depend on God. The finances I used to have were gone. Many of the friends I thought I had were gone. Yet God became my daily bread. He remained close, and He remained real when nothing else was making sense. Because of His hand on my life I matured enough to see that my hope was never supposed to be in my husband, friends, or church members but in God alone. When I truly understood this, I learned to love and forgive those who betrayed and hurt me.

God is at work in our lives even when we can't see Him. As I've said before, He knows the ending of everyone's story before the beginning. We have learned to trust what we can see and feel, but God wants us to trust Him and His Word.

God may be invisible, but He is always invincible. He is present in every scene and movement of our days. Humans can see only a fraction of the light spectrum while honeybees and homing pigeons can detect ultraviolet light that is invisible to us.[7] In the supernatural realm, our vision is even more limited. We get only occasional glimpses of that unseen world. It follows then that our inability to see the activity of God does not mean He is not working in our lives.

If you ever feel God is silent or hidden in your life, remember Esther's story and the words of 2 Corinthians 5:7: "We walk by faith, not by sight" (KJV). Never doubt the presence and activity of God! In 2 Kings 6, the king of Aram surrounded Israel with his army, and it seemed as though the people were doomed. The servant of the prophet Elisha looked out at the vast army and cried out, "What are we going to do?" The prophet wasn't moved. He told the servant to fear not, and he asked the Lord to open the man's eyes. When the servant was able to see in the spirit realm, he saw the hillside was filled with horses and chariots of fire.

There were more troops with Israel than against them. The same is true for you and me. No matter what is happening in our lives, there are more with us than against us. Let me say that again. God has more supernatural warriors fighting for us than Satan has fighting against us. We are children of the Most High God, and He will never forsake us. He allows these seasons to strengthen us as we learn to depend on Him.

OBEDIENCE IS BETTER THAN SACRIFICE

There are many different types and symbols in the Bible. In the Book of Esther, Mordecai is a type of the Holy Spirit. A comforter is one called to walk alongside someone to offer help or counsel. Every day Mordecai walked in front of the palace to see how Esther was doing and to give her instruction. Even though her position had changed, she still obeyed her cousin. Likewise, the Holy Spirit will go before us each day to lead us and guide us if we will obey Him.

Esther could have responded to being in the palace in a number of ways. She could have thought of her circumstances as luck or an entitlement occasioned by her beauty, or that she somehow had a hand in bringing about her ascension. After twelve months of beautification treatments and living in the lap of luxury, she could have ignored Mordecai when he told her of the edict to kill the Jews. She could have ignored her God-given assignment. Unfortunately this happens all too often in the body of Christ.

People go through a valley experience and God transforms and promotes them, but they forget why God brought them out of their low season. When things are going well, it is common for people to think God will ask someone else to sacrifice to help others. We must never forget that God blesses us so we can be a blessing. To whom much is given, much is required (Luke 12:48).

Despite the risk of execution Esther fulfilled God's calling on her life. She chose not to hide behind her comfortable position as queen and her comfort in the palace. We must do the same. We must be willing to become living sacrifices unto God and remember that this life is not about us. It is about the advancement of the kingdom of God. Worship leader William McDowell said it well in his song "I Give Myself Away."

Here I am
Here I stand
Lord, my life is in Your hands
Lord, I'm longing to see
Your desires revealed in me
I give myself away.

Take my heart
Take my life
As a living sacrifice
All my dreams, all my plans
Lord, I place them in Your hands.

My life is not my own,
To Him I belong
I give myself, I give myself away
So You can use me.[8]

We must give ourselves away so God can use us. Our lives don't belong to us; they belong to Him.

This song beautifully expresses how Esther reacted to her situation. She said, "If I perish, I perish," because she knew her life was in God's hands. You too must know your life is in the hands of an everlasting God. Trust Him to take care of you in your valley experience, and be obedient to His voice.

INCREASED ANOINTING

The story of Esther is just one example in Scripture of how disadvantageous circumstances can make us stronger and increase our spiritual authority. Esther became queen "for such a time as this"—for the purpose of delivering the Jews from genocide (Esther 4:14). That calling forced her to put her life at risk, but that is why she was chosen. She was called to stand in the gap for her people. That was the plan and purpose of God for Esther's life.

Jacob, one of the great patriarchs of the Christian faith, experienced a long valley experience. He earned a reputation as a charlatan, was tricked by his father-in-law into marrying a woman he didn't love, and spent years evading his older brother Esau, who wanted to kill him for stealing his birthright. Jacob felt far from God and wrestled with an angel for an entire night just to be blessed. Unlike Esther, Jacob made most of the messes he found himself in. But Jacob's trials actually cultivated him into a man who was pleasing in the sight of God.

David, one of the most well-known figures in the Bible, was a man who experienced great pain. His life was rife with rejection, betrayal, sin, and loss. After God anointed David king, a man he once admired, King Saul, became so jealous that he hunted David down and tried several times to kill him. Yet God repeatedly protected David and would not allow anything to keep him from fulfilling his destiny.

Many of you reading this book may have experienced a friend's betrayal, the death of a family member, loss of financial freedom, illness, or some other painful trial. I want to you to know God has a purpose for the trial. He will use it to make you better. I encourage you to ask your-self three questions: What did I learn from this trial? What did I gain from this trial? And how did this trial make me better?

Let me give you my answers to those questions. I learned that my life was never attached to a person; my life, destiny, and purpose were always wrapped in God, my Creator. As a result, I am not a slave to man's opinion of me.

I gained an undeniable strength in God, as well as authority and confidence to overcome the enemy. And I am now able to tap into gifts and talents I didn't realize I had. My trial made me so much better, because I learned to truly respect and love myself as a royal child of the Most High God. Today I can love others more freely.

So instead of asking "Why me?" when the waves of life begin to crash and the storm clouds begin to gather overhead, realize that God has ordained a purpose for the pain, a reason for the resistance, and a testimony to be brought forth from the trial. Give yourself away to God, and you will not return empty-handed or empty-hearted.

CHAPTER
3

PROCESSING
THE PAIN

The five stages of grief psychiatrist Elisabeth Kübler-Ross introduced in the late 1960s are well known and nearly universally accepted. Grief, however, does not always follow a linear pattern and manifests itself in varied iterations, phases, and intensities. Grief does not necessarily include all of Kübler-Ross's stages of denial, anger, bargaining, depression, and acceptance. Different people experience and process grief in different ways.

No matter how you experience grief, I cannot express emphatically enough how important it is that you process the pain. Though I went through the classic five stages of grief, I did not experience them in any particular order. I would go a couple of days feeling great and thinking my pain was over, then without warning a wave of grief would hit me so hard it would leave me bedridden. There were also triggers that would set me off—the name of a city or person, a song, or even a month in the year that rekindled the pain of my husband's betrayal. Even the most insignificant, inconspicuous reminder would dredge up renewed heartache.

Skilled counselors can't make the pain go away, but they can help a person process their grief in a healthy way. Unfortunately I did not realize the kind of counseling I needed and turned to people who did not give me the opportunity to fully process the pain I felt. I remember an incident that occurred soon after my husband's infidelity became public. I was traveling with my husband to attend a conference that was supposed to aid in our healing process.

On the plane he dropped yet another bombshell about one of his affairs, briefing me on a previously unknown incident. I felt like I was dying all over again. I had become extremely frail, and after hearing this news, I didn't know whether I would be able to stand. I managed to keep my composure at the airport, but when we arrived in our hotel room, I began vomiting uncontrollably. The conference began that night, and I couldn't keep anything down.

When my husband informed the couple hosting the conference that I wouldn't be able to attend, the wife called me and told me I needed to come. Crying, I explained to her that I could barely stand and was very sick. What I had learned on the plane devastated me. She proceeded to tell me that she had dealt with infidelity in her marriage, and I basically needed to get over it and come to the conference. Her cold words and lack of compassion cut me like a knife. I felt even more alone than I did when I arrived. I thought the conference would be a comfort to both of us, but that was not the case. Zach went to the conference without me while I lay in the room sick.

Like physical injuries, emotional wounds become less painful over time. But grieving is a natural part of the healing process. It is one of the body's natural coping mechanisms. Denying or delaying grief can hinder your immune system and diminish your emotional strength.[1] There were times when I deliberately avoided grieving because, quite frankly, I was afraid it would hurt too much. This avoidance caused the grief to get bottled up deep inside me. Over time it took a gallant effort just to suppress the grief, and I eventually became numb to life.

I remember a specific occasion when I was invited to be the guest speaker at a church's anniversary. The pastors of this church are extremely dear to me because their ministry was birthed out of the church my husband and I founded. This was my second or third speaking engagement since Zach and I separated, and as I stood behind the pulpit to minister, I was ready to release an apostolic and prophetic word. But when I looked at the congregation, I saw people I knew from the church I had co-pastored with my husband, and I could no longer concentrate. The words just fumbled out of my mouth.

I had been speaking for less than fifteen minutes when I looked at my notes and saw nothing but blank paper. Although the notes were there, in my embarrassment and shame I couldn't focus on the words on the page. I saw faces looking at me with sorrow and even disappointment. All I could do was apologize as I walked away from the pulpit.

Everyone stared at me as I left the sanctuary and eventually the building in abject humiliation. This was the most embarrassing thing that had ever happened to me. Why did God allow me to fail in such a public way? I already had naysayers, and now they were gloating. What did I do to deserve such a horrible outcome? I wanted to die.

As my friend was driving me home, I wanted to cry. I was convincing myself the experience was an obvious sign that I would never minister again. I thought about moving to the West Coast, where I would never see or be seen by anyone I knew. My healing process was not complete.

We were almost home when I asked my friend what I could have done differently. She said, "You could have stayed." I realized she was right, so I told her to turn the car around. I had to face the humiliation head-on. When I reentered the sanctuary, what I saw literally took my breath away. The church leaders and visiting pastors had gathered on the pulpit and were praying intently for me. Almost everyone on the pulpit had come from the church Zach and I founded.

They embraced me and apologized for not covering me in prayer during the most painful time of my life. They realized that while their lives had gone on in the two years since my husband's infidelity was exposed, I was still very much in the throes of a divorce. They began to cover me in prayer, prophesying over and encouraging me. I felt strengthened. I felt loved. I felt accepted. I felt understood, and I felt covered.

There are times in our lives when we must face the pain of the process. Had I not gone back to face the pain, I would not have been blessed. Had

I not shown my frailties as I grieved the loss of my marriage, I would have been in danger of becoming dysfunctional. I may have tried to avoid people, difficult situations, and ultimately life. My ability to foster new relationships would have been hindered. Had I held in all the pain and not channeled it properly, I probably would have experienced an emotional collapse.

Everyone processes grief differently, but it is imperative that you deal with the pain properly. There are some highly anointed people in church who can pray for you and preach to you, but they may not be able to help you process grief. As well-meaning as they may be, if they are not equipped to help you walk through the grieving process, they will do more harm than good. I often wonder whether my marriage would have survived had we received the proper counseling right at the beginning.

Just as everyone gives and accepts love differently, so too do people process their pain differently. What is most important is that we deal with the pain because God wants to use that process to transform us and make us more like Christ. He wants us to become beacons of light and hope for others going through a painful transition.

TRANSITION LEADS TO TRANSFORMATION

We make transitions throughout our lives. We transition from preschool to kindergarten, from high school to college, from childhood to adulthood, from being single to being married. Life is a series of transitions from one state to the next. Transitioning can be easy and exciting, such as a high school graduation or the birth of a child. Transitions can also be very difficult, such as a midlife crisis or divorce. But no matter how painful it is, we must embrace the transition process so we can experience transformation.

Whether calculated or unanticipated, transitions provide rich potential for transformation. In this chapter I want to discuss the kind of painful transition that requires every ounce of mental strength to make the tough calls and press past one's own will to experience transformation.

The definition of *transition* is "passage from one state, stage, subject, or place to another; a movement, development, or evolution from one form, stage, or style to another."[2] A *process* is "a continuous action, operation, or series of changes taking place in a definite manner."[3] In order to successfully transition, we must understand the dynamics of processing pain. If we are not able to process the pain in a valley season, our transition phase may be prolonged. I don't want that for you. Hosea 4:6 says God's people perish for a lack of knowledge. I don't want you to perish; I want you to learn what I wish I had known during my transition so you can survive and overcome.

My world was literally turned upside down when my husband and I separated. I lost my position at the church and had to move into a smaller home. After spending fourteen years building a church and raising a family, I felt I had nothing to show for my hard work. I lapsed into depression. In my despair I often gazed at the lot across the street from my home. It was empty, with no trees, no flowers, no grass—nothing. The only thing on the lot was the foundation for a house to be built. I made a correlation between that empty lot and my life. I felt empty and reduced to nothing, yet I still had a foundation in my relationship with God.

Emotionally I was in limbo. Though not in agony anymore, I still hurt. I had begun the process of forgiving, but I had not been made whole. I was still dealing with the pain.

The person who led my husband to the Lord and mentored him in the things of God, Pastor Douglas Chukwuemeka, was extremely hurt by Zach's actions. Yet he and his wife, Roslyn, showed unconditional love and support to both of us. After Zach's infidelity was exposed, Pastor Doug and Roslyn often made it a point to call and encourage me. They spoke words of life and wisdom to my soul and spirit. During one of our conversations Pastor Doug shared a concept he was learning about in his psychology courses called "liminality."

Anthropologist Victor Turner helped develop the concept of liminality and explained it in an essay titled "Betwixt and Between." Significant transitions in life involve the passage through what Turner called a liminal experience. The word *liminal* comes from the Latin term *limen*, which refers to the threshold of a doorway. It is an in-between state when you're neither here nor there. A liminal experience brings radical disorientation and confusion. The rules of what you have known don't apply anymore, nor do the rules of the place into which you're headed. It is a time of great uncertainty and insecurity.[4]

Drawing from the concept of liminality and my experience of being in limbo during the two years my husband and I were separated but not divorced, I have identified three stages we go through when processing pain in times of transition.

SEPARATION/ENDING STAGE

The separation stage begins when something ends. There are thousands upon thousands of scenarios of this stage. The separation stage starts when a loved one dies, someone retires, or a church grows and loses its small-church identity. During this ending stage, there is no turning back. It's when you are full-term and the labor pains start. It's when you say, "I do," or when you sign the divorce papers. It's when you resign from your job, take that step to skydive out of an airplane, or receive anesthesia before a surgery. Even if you don't like it, you can't go back to the way things were when you're in the separation stage.

My dear friend Alicia, who pastored a church with her husband in New York, went through an ending stage. Her husband unexpectedly fell ill, and she rushed him to the emergency room. The physicians diagnosed him as having influenza and prescribed antibiotics, but the diagnosis turned out to be wrong. He actually had meningitis, and because it wasn't treated properly, my friend's husband died.

As you can imagine, this was a devastating ending stage in Alicia's life. This happened around the same time my marriage was ending, and we were experiencing very similar emotions. I watched Alicia go through the weight loss, the stress of dealing with lawyers, the erosion of her finances. I could see how much she longed to return to the life she had known, to feel her husband's touch and hear his voice. But she could not reclaim those things.

The disciples experienced the ending stage when Jesus ascended into heaven. Jesus had led them through a whirlwind of incredible experiences. He had been their leader, teacher, mentor, and friend for three and a half years. The disciples had always been able to rely on Jesus to fix whatever they messed up. It was like having a real-live superhero as a confidant.

For three and a half years they were able to observe Jesus, live with Him, and fellowship with Him. Then, in a matter of minutes, He was gone to be with our heavenly Father. The disciples were understandably overcome with grief. The Scriptures say their hearts were filled with sorrow (John 16:6), which is a perfectly normal and healthy response to losing someone dear. Jesus tried to convince the disciples that they would actually benefit from His departure. "I tell you the truth. It is to your advantage that I go away" (John 16:7, NKJV). But His words could do only so much to relieve their sadness.

The ending/separation stage can be paralyzing for those who lose a loved one. It is devastating when people who are supposed to be in your life forever are suddenly gone. The void they leave can be insufferably painful. How could God work something like this to our advantage?

In addition to the emptiness and agony of yearning for a lost loved one, the separation/ending stage can bring a ton of new responsibilities. My husband had always taken care of everything financial. Even before the divorce was final, I had to obtain health insurance, which is extremely difficult for someone who has no job. I had to get car insurance, look for employment, balance a household budget, and still care for four children.

Because I was still grieving the loss of my marriage, these responsibilities seemed virtually impossible to manage. I kept hearing God say, "Breakthrough is inevitable." But I was totally unable to comprehend what He meant by that.

The separation/ending stage causes feelings of insecurity, isolation, profound loss, and emptiness. The fact that there is no turning back only makes those feelings harder to bear. So what are we to do next? When life changes course and we find ourselves in an ending/separation phase, how do we process this loss and the resulting pain?

RESPONDING STAGE

The responding stage is the knee-jerk reaction to the ending stage. It is also the phase that leads to liminality, or that place of limbo, and then transition. The responding stage is loaded with a myriad of emotions, ranging from shock to grief to anger and depression. This plethora of emotions often causes people to either become numb or, on the other extreme, go haywire.

The 1996 movie *A Time to Kill* depicted a classic example of the responding stage. The movie, based on John Grisham's 1989 novel of the same name, chronicles a young white lawyer named Jake Brigance (played by Matthew McConaughey) who defends a black man named Carl Lee Hailey (played by Samuel L. Jackson) on trial for murdering two white men who savagely beat and raped his ten-year-old daughter. The pain of his daughter's attack caused Hailey to snap mentally and publicly gun down the rapists.

The television show *Snapped* broadcasts true stories of people who mentally collapse under pressure and do horrible things they normally would not do. They render permanent solutions to temporary problems. I've seen couples destroy their fine china out of anger and then regret it later. Others send incriminating e-mails or text messages to hurt a friend or spouse without first considering that they can never take back those actions or words.

Recently a mother from Tampa, Florida, was jailed for shooting her two teenage children because they talked back to her.[5] We have heard about husbands murdering their wives to receive life insurance benefits because of financial pressures. Even more devastating, children who have been subject to bullying are increasingly turning to murder or suicide for relief. In the responding stage, rational judgment is often clouded and foresight is blinded, causing us to rely on our emotions for guidance. The responding stage, if we are not careful, can be deadly.

I am reminded of the Persuaders's 1971 song "Thin Line Between Love and Hate."

It's five o'clock in the morning, and I'm just getting in
I knock on the door
A voice sweet and low say, "Who is it?"
She opens up the door and lets me in
Never once does she asks, "Where have you been?"
She says, "Are you hungry, honey, did you eat yet?"
"Let me hang up your coat," the woman tells me. "Pass me your hat."
All the time she's smiling, never raises her voice
It's five o'clock in the morning
And I don't give it a second thought
Don't think you can keep breaking your woman's heart
And she'll sit back and enjoy it.
The sweetest woman in the world
Could be the meanest woman in the world
If you make her that way
You keep hurting her, she'll keep being quiet
She might be holding something inside
That'll really, really hurt you one day
Here I am laying in the hospital
Bandaged from feet to head
In a state of shock
Just that much from being dead
I didn't think my woman
Would do something like this to me
Didn't think my girl had the nerve
Here I am, I guess action speaks louder than words
Don't think you can keep treating your woman bad
And she won't ever get mad.[6]

You may be wondering if I "snapped" or went completely haywire when I found out my husband had been unfaithful. The answer is yes and no. I snapped inwardly. I lost trust for everyone except God, my family, and close friends. I harbored hatred toward my husband and several others who I felt let me down. I came dangerously close to the point where I really didn't care anymore. I thank God my experience wasn't any worse.

One of the worst things we can do is to make a permanent decision during a temporary situation. Our first reaction to pain is not always the best one. When we have to process heartache, the Holy Spirit always beckons us to walk by His Spirit and not according to the flesh (Gal. 5:16–17). Our first response is usually something our flesh motivates us to do. The Holy Spirit will challenge us to be spiritually minded, which brings life and peace (Rom. 8:6–10). Our flesh will tell us to do things that cause us to hurt ourselves or others, but the Bible says we are to be slow to wrath (James 1:19).

If it weren't for my dear friends and family, my responding stage could have been very self-destructive. At one point I had it in my mind to remarry right away. I believed wholeheartedly that God was going to bless me with a tall, dark, handsome man who looked like Idris Elba, and all of my pain would disappear. I reasoned that I was a great wife and mother, and I deserved to finally be happy with someone who would cherish me.

My desire to move quickly into another relationship was a result of anxiety and fear. I thought I didn't have much time to work with. I was almost forty years old at the time and had four children, and my oldest son has special needs. I wasn't sure anyone would want to marry me then, but I figured my chances would only grow slimmer with time. Obviously I was not in my right mind. I was in the responding stage and reacting badly to my new, unwanted situation.

From all appearances, my husband seemed to be enjoying life. He seemed invigorated while I was devastated. His attitude brought on feelings of rejection and made me want to find someone to love and accept me even more. We know this type of behavior is called "rebounding," which can be a volatile emotional place for women and men alike. When a loved one dies or a relationship disintegrates, people become vulnerable. The allure of being "with" someone or not feeling rejected causes many to search for love in all the wrong places.

When we are most vulnerable, often the enemy will send traps to lure us into sin. Because of decisions they made during the responding stage, some people end up prematurely remarried, engaging in fornication, resigning from a good job or ministry position, or returning to an unhealthy relationship. I will discuss this more extensively in chapter 5.

I didn't have any single male friends, so I constantly surfed social networks looking to reconnect with old friends. I was interested in anyone interested in me. To God be the glory, I could not find anyone. My next venture was an online dating site. Again no one met my requirements.

Then that December I received a brief text from a single pastor wishing me a merry Christmas and happy New Year. A dear friend of mine had given him my number. At that point in my life I had no interest in pastors and had no desire to pursue a romantic relationship with this minister. But he lived in a different state, so we began to develop a friendship via telephone.

I enjoyed being able to talk freely with him, and I found myself releasing some of my pain. I even tried to match him up with one of my beautiful, single friends. However, it wasn't long before I actually started to have feelings toward this pastor because he presented me with earthly security. He was financially stable, had a ministry in need of a first lady, wasn't opposed to dating someone with children, and did not reject me.

Unbeknownst to me, a third party began reading the e-mails I exchanged with this pastor. I was mortified to say the least. But all things work together for the good of those who love the Lord and are called according to His purpose. Because of the embarrassing intrusion, I pulled back from that long-distance friendship. Although I did not realize it at the time, pursuing a romantic relationship with the pastor would have taken me off my path to becoming whole. I would have made a permanent decision in my temporary pain. I was nowhere near ready for a relationship with anyone. I still needed to go through the healing process.

TRANSITION/LIMINAL STAGE

The responding stage leads to the transition/liminal stage. This is literally like being in limbo. You are no longer in the responding stage, but you haven't completed your transition. Liminality is characterized by ambiguity. During this phase what was once your reality no longer exists. Your sense of identity dissolves to some extent, and you are left in a state of bewilderment. The limits you normally would have put on your thoughts and behavior are more relaxed. And because you yearn for more out of life, a part of you is open to something new.

It's like being on a roller-coaster ride. As the car cranks slowly up the track, your chest heaves and your heart pounds because you know something is coming. You feel exhilarated but simultaneously very frightened because you know the big drop is ahead, and the only thing holding you in place is a small, somewhat insignificant bar and, if you're lucky, a seat belt.

Then when you reach the apex of the coaster, the world seems to go quiet for a minute. Everything seems to pause. You know, however, that you cannot stay in that moment forever. You know more is coming. You are open to something new yet anxious because you don't know exactly what is ahead. This is what it means to be in liminality. You have left one stage but have not completed your transition into the next phase.

My liminal stage lasted two years. Though not yet divorced, my husband and I were separated. The legal process was absolutely brutal. I could not move forward, and I did not want to go backward. I often said it felt like not being able to walk on solid ground. I felt no security. Nothing was solid in my life except Jesus. I no longer had a job, church home, ministry, or husband. I didn't know who I was or who I was to become.

A great metaphor for this phase is the transformation of a caterpillar into a butterfly. In the chrysalis, which is often mistakenly called a cocoon, the caterpillar's entire being is broken down into disassociated mush. The mush is neither caterpillar nor butterfly. If you were to open the chrysalis and look at the mush stage, the creature would be unidentifiable. But the butterfly eventually develops from these components.[7]

The mush phase is the butterfly's liminal/transition stage, a time when one state of being has been demolished but the new has not yet been constructed. Adolescence is another example of liminality. An adolescent is no longer a child, but she is not yet an adult. Parents will admonish an adolescent to stop acting like a child then almost in the same breath say she is not ready to make adult decisions. Engaged couples too are in the liminal stage. They are committed to each other with a ring serving as proof of their bond, but they are not yet married.

It is the liminal stage that brings frustration, especially when you are processing pain. God often requires us to wait on Him while we continue to ache. Waiting on the Lord is a matter of determined faith. Waiting on the Lord does not mean doing nothing. It literally means we serve Him as a waiter or waitress would serve patrons at a restaurant. As believers we each must serve God to the best of our ability.

There were times during my liminal stage when I envied unbelievers. It seemed as though non-Christians kept excelling while I was being tormented. At some points I even contemplated backsliding. But when I committed to continue serving the Lord by remaining faithful in prayer, worship, and fellowshiping with other believers, thoughts of backsliding began to evaporate.

Why is the liminal/transition stage so important? Because this is when God allows the birthing process to begin. This is the beginning stage of the manifestation of your breakthrough. It is the start of your transformation.

Any mother can attest to the fact that the birthing process is extremely painful. The medical term for the stage between contractions and actual delivery is called "transition." You can't get from labor to birth without it. Transition is the brief time when the baby is still firmly within the womb yet unmistakably ready to come out. When women describe this stage, for which there is little coaching, they usually say this is the most difficult time of birth.

Midwives often joke that transition is the moment when women decide they really didn't want to have a baby after all! They have a strong physical and mental desire to keep the baby safely where it has been for nine months. Yet they have an equally irresistible urge to push the baby out into the waiting world. In the birth process transition is that scary time when two equally powerful forces meet. You have the desire to keep things as they are and the compulsion to move toward new birth.

When we are in a valley season, the liminal phase is designed to birth in us something stronger and better, such as self-respect, joy, peace, and compassion. It could be a business, ministry, or even a better marriage. Unfortunately the pain of transition causes many to become tired and discouraged. I have seen people experience trial after trial after trial—until they have no more strength left.

I experienced this with the birth of my youngest daughter. I had literally gone twenty-four hours without sleep and was in agonizing pain the entire time. When it was finally time for me to push, I had no strength left. I begged the doctor to perform a C-section. But she was adamant that it was too late for that procedure and said my daughter's life would be in danger if I did not push immediately. My thoughts drifted to my oldest son, who was born with cerebral palsy. I didn't want to put my baby in danger. I cried as I asked the doctor if she could use forceps to pull the baby out. Again she told me it would be too dangerous. When I thought my daughter's health was in jeopardy, I mustered every bit of strength I had to push.

Imagine experiencing financial blow after financial blow or repeated infidelity. If there is no relief, you will eventually lose strength and think you cannot press forward. A woman I know went through a trial identical to mine. However, when she reached the liminal/transition stage, she had no more strength to fight. So she went back to the lifestyle she lived before she got saved. She entertained quite a few men, consumed alcohol liberally, and resumed smoking marijuana. Her life soon spiraled out of control. This was especially sad to see because the breakup of her marriage wasn't her fault. She fell into the enemy's snare. Praise the Lord, she is walking with God again, but she could have avoided a painful detour.

How could a woman who was a leader in her church fall into such a trap? Why would she go back to an ungodly lifestyle? Of course people fall into sin for different reasons. However, I believe one of the major reasons Christians fall for the enemy's traps is because we begin to doubt God and His Word. When we are in the midst of a trial, battle fatigue often sets in, causing us to focus more on our dilemma than the solution.

A WAY IN THE WILDERNESS

The Bible says in Exodus 3:9 that God heard the cry of His people, who were being enslaved in Egypt. So He elevated Moses to lead the children of Israel out of four hundred years of bondage. God performed astounding miracles, including turning water into blood and parting the Red Sea. But coming out of Egypt was just the beginning. The children of Israel were ready to be free, but they were not ready to go through the pain of their transition. Although they saw the supernatural miracles of God, they longed for the familiar. They wanted the leeks and the onions they ate in Egypt (Num. 11:5). The children of Israel made several mistakes during their transition/liminal stage that we would be wise to avoid.

Don't complain.

The Israelites began murmuring and complaining when they saw giants in the land God had promised them (Num. 14:1–3). They didn't realize that by focusing on the giants, they weren't focusing on God's promise. Murmuring and complaining will take your attention off God. Praise and worship will do just the opposite. What you focus on will determine your direction. If you focus on the past, you will not move forward. If you focus on God, you will receive all you need to obtain the promise.

Don't choose the familiar.

Although the children of Israel were free from the bondage of Egypt, they were walking in circles because they still had a slave mentality. I often see men and women who are unable to move forward because they are stuck in their pain and don't know how to let the Lord heal them. Countless people return to what is familiar instead of pressing toward the unknown. They doubt that God could change their circumstances, especially if they have seen corruption in the church. Only Jesus can heal our hurts.

You will never move forward if you hold on to the past. It is unhealthy, for instance, to keep all the belongings of a deceased loved one. Some people never touch the room of the deceased. Others constantly look at pictures or videos of their loved one. After you've given yourself time to grieve, you must move forward; otherwise you will rob yourself of the opportunity to live to the fullest the life God gave you.

Don't let your past dictate your future.

One of the worst hurts is church hurt. I used to think and even say that all preachers were the same—even though I knew wonderful men and women of God who were full of integrity. Because of my hurt, I became skeptical of everyone in ministry. I based my perceptions of church leaders on the pain I experienced. This happens to different people in different ways. Some women who have been mistreated by men say all men are dogs. Some even turn to lesbianism because they never processed their pain. Other people may stereotype an ethnic group because of painful past experiences. But the ironic thing is, God uses the unexpected and the unconventional to bless us. He may use the very race you said you disliked to move you deeper into your purpose. If we refuse to release wounds from the past, we will become imprisoned by our pain and never experience all God has for us.

Don't fake the process; embrace it.

I have been known to say, "You have to fake it until you make it," but that's not always true. We can say we forgive someone, but unless our fruit matches what we have said, our words mean nothing. We must be careful not to give lip service. When we ask someone how he is doing, we expect to hear something positive. You've probably heard people respond with the popular phrase, "I am blessed and highly favored." But most of us would probably be surprised to hear someone say, "I am downtrodden and desperately oppressed."

There is a place for speaking words of life into our situation, but there is a balance to strike. We are not to deny the pain we are experiencing. We need to be willing to share our struggles with loving Christians so they can lift us up in prayer and we can be healed (James 5:16). And we must become the kind of Christians who would be ready to lend an ear and a helping hand when someone comes to us with their struggles.

During times of transition our pain can feel unbearable, but we aren't supposed to process it all at once. How do you eat an elephant? One bite at a time. Overwhelming hurt can be paralyzing. When it seems like the whole world is against you, that is not the time to try to absorb all of your problems.

At the beginning of my trial, my mind would never shut off. I could sleep for only two hours a night. I remember getting in the car during those sleepless nights and driving aimlessly while my mind idled in "neutral." I finally learned to allow everything to occur in its due season (Eccles. 3:1); then I found rest in the Lord. We are taught patience through the storms.

Don't give up in the transition stage. Don't lose hope and faith. Gather all the strength you can muster to PUSH (pray until something happens). Hebrews 12:2 says we should "fix our eyes on Jesus, the author and perfecter of our faith, who for the joy set before him endured the cross, scorning its shame, and sat down at the right hand of the throne of God." The same love Jesus showed for mankind when He endured the cross is the same love God has for us today. But you must exercise faith. Jesus said, "If you have faith as small as a mustard seed, you can say to this mulberry tree, 'Be uprooted and planted in the sea,' and it will obey you" (Luke 17:6).

REASSIMILATION

God's plan is to transform us into the image of His Son in this life. Part of this process includes going into the wilderness, where we are alone or feel deserted. We will talk more about this in the next chapter. The wilderness represents the season of life when we discover for ourselves who we are and who God is. Jesus told Nicodemus, "God did not send his Son into the world to condemn the world, but in order that the world might be saved through him" (John 3:17, ESV). Similarly God does not send us into the wilderness to punish or destroy us but to free us from the snares that would stop us from obtaining the promises He made to us.

When we complete the transition process by correctly processing the pain, we are transformed into new creations empowered by God's strength and grace. Our light shines in the midst of darkness and confusion. We have a sure peace and understanding of God's loving-kindness. When we are hurting, we can easily hurt others by operating from our pain. But after we pass the test or trial, we no longer run that risk. God, therefore, allows us to reassimilate into our positions in life, often with a promotion.

CHAPTER 4

HELP! IS ANYBODY OUT THERE?

I've learned through the painful process of transitioning for transformation that God allows us to be alone at times. The Word of God tells us that the Spirit of the Lord led Jesus into the wilderness, where He was tempted by the devil (Matt. 4:1). For a season God will seemingly isolate us from the rest of humanity, but He has a purpose for this time. In this season God teaches us to depend on Him. It is a time when recent wounds can be dressed and past scars healed. It is a season designed to increase our faith that God is, and has always been, sovereign.

We read in the Book of Genesis that Joseph endured a season such as this. He was betrayed by his brothers, thrown into a pit, sold into slavery, and put in prison (Gen. 37). Yet in the wilderness of his isolation Joseph trusted God, who in turn lifted Joseph up, in spirit and in stature, to heights he could have only imagined. But while in the pit, while in his prison cell, Joseph endured a very lonely place.

It's not that no one wanted to help Joseph. After his brothers cast Joseph into the pit, one brother, Reuben, returned to get Joseph out, but slave traders had already taken him captive (Gen. 37:29). The fact is, sometimes people can't help you. And that is by design. In the wilderness God will sever all lifelines but His own.

In these wilderness seasons, nobody answers you, no matter how hard or how loud you cry, "Help!" God places you between the proverbial rock and a hard place. I'm not talking about just an inconvenient situation. We have all needed someone to pick up the kids because we were running late, or bring us some gas because we ran out, or even give us a boost into an open window after we locked the keys in the house. But none of those are truly examples of being lodged between a rock and a hard place.

When you are between a rock and a hard place, the situation is so bad no earthly person can help you. It is when the test results are so dire your doctor can't look you in the eye. It is when you discover irrefutable evidence of your spouse's infidelity. It is when your child's drug habit lands him in the hospital or a jail cell. When you're between a rock and a hard place, your hands are tied and you can't do anything to change the situation. It is when you look to your mother and all she can say is, "It's gonna be all right, baby."

When you're between a rock and a hard place, you notice people start distancing themselves from you. Your pastor stops answering the phone and the people you thought would come and see about you are nowhere to be found. It is during these times that you are officially in the middle of the wilderness.

Desperation is always lurking in the shadows of the wilderness. Desperation is brought on by circumstances with which the mind struggles to cope. Desperation produces despondency, where the constant crashing of life's waves causes a person to become disassociated from the world around him, unable to tell one blow from the next.

There were days when I would lie in bed in complete silence, unable to eat or sleep. I would just stare at the ceiling, barely able to form the words to pray. I got to the point where I didn't care whether tomorrow came. Hope was fading, like candlelight when the flame reaches the end of its wick. It took all the strength I had just to make it through the day.

I don't know what I would have done without my children. They kept me alive. I knew I had to be there to give them hope because they were hurting too.

But what about those who don't have young children to keep them in their right mind? When a person is trapped between a rock and a hard place, he can easily feel like a caged animal that is being poked, prodded, and provoked by onlookers. When animals (and people in many cases) feel threatened and have no way of escape, even the most docile creature may lash out violently. I have learned that hurting people hurt people. When stuck between a rock and a hard place, with no one available or able to help, people often do things they never imagined themselves doing.

When we take the time to evaluate many Christians' dysfunctional behavior, more often than not the root cause is a traumatic wilderness experience that left lasting pain, bitterness, and shame. Instead of leaning on the Spirit of the Lord to provide the necessary provision, they leaned on their flesh. They followed the ways of the world in an effort to cope with the pain. As a result the body of Christ ends up with Christians whose lives don't reflect the fruit of Spirit but rather the pride of life and the lust of the eyes—all because they did not submit to the purging process of the wilderness.

In the Book of Genesis, Jacob repeatedly resorted to manipulation and deception to gain what he desired. He manipulated his older brother, Esau, into giving him his birthright. He tricked his father into giving him Esau's blessing. Fortunately for Jacob and for us, God didn't look at Jacob and see only who he was; He saw who Jacob was to become. He saw the diamond in the rough and knew what Jacob needed in order to reach his potential.

In Genesis 28 Jacob was traveling from Beersheeba to Haran, running from his brother, who was trying to kill him for stealing his birthright. As he journeyed, night began to overtake him, and unable to find lodging, Jacob slept in the wilderness using stones as pillows. God positioned Jacob between a rock and a hard place, where he could not call on anyone for help except God.

While Jacob slept, God spoke prophetically to him in a dream. The Lord told Jacob that his offspring would be like the dust of the earth and that the land he was lying on would one day be his. Most important, perhaps, God promised Jacob that He would always be with him. When Jacob awoke, he said, "Surely the LORD is in this place, and I was not aware of it" (Gen. 28:16). In the wilderness, God found Jacob. In the wilderness, Jacob found God. When God takes us into the wilderness, the best thing we can do is follow Jacob's example and rest our head on the Rock, who is God.

THE ROCK REVEALS YOUR DESTINY AND PURPOSE

When you are between a rock and a hard place, resting your head on the Rock will allow God to speak to your purpose and destiny. When you rest your head on the Rock, God will relieve your anxious mind. When you rest on the Rock, you surrender your will and dismiss your agenda. You allow God to penetrate your hardened exterior and give you direction.

This is also when God will speak to you. God told Jacob his descendants would be like the dust of the earth, and all peoples on earth would be blessed through him and his offspring (Gen. 28:14). At the time Jacob was unmarried and in the process of running from his brother, who wanted to kill him for stealing his birthright. God is amazing. He seldom speaks to your current situation; He usually speaks to your future.

While in your wilderness experience you may be struggling to come up with this month's rent or have mere pennies in the bank. But that is when God will declare that you will be a millionaire. How is that possible? Even when there seems to be no earthly way, God's Word will bring you hope and peace that surpass natural understanding.

A dear friend of mine is a senior prophetess. During my lowest moments she would speak words of promise to me. The prophetic words became a defibrillator that sent voltage to my spiritual heart. Those words of life kept me spiritually alive. In the natural I had been hurting for so long I could not imagine life without that pain. But the words of promise brought hope that there would be a new day. We talked almost every day. My friend literally became a daily lifeline for me. I thank God she was patient enough to let me tell her about my problems and my pain over and over and over. She is a true friend.

With my hope renewed, I developed a desire to get my fight back. I didn't allow hopelessness to rule my day. I meditated on the life-giving Word of God and the prophetic words spoken to me as I rested my head on the Rock.

I began to understand why after being rejected and ostracized, the ten lepers in Luke 17:12–13 refused to give up and die. They cried out to Jesus for mercy, and He healed them. God is attracted to weakness. He hears the cries of the desperate.

God allows us to be broken so He can remake us in His image. We may have believed it when someone said we weren't smart enough, pretty enough, anointed enough, or talented enough. But when we wake up after resting on the Rock, we can better discern the enemy's lies.

I was the perfect victim crying, "Help! Can anybody hear me?" I wanted people to sympathize and empathize with me. I felt helpless and defeated. I wanted to figure out what was so horribly wrong with me that I would experience such betrayal. My focus was on my insecurities and myself until the dreams and prophetic words God gave me began to scream, "Wake up!" Once awake I could see things as they really were. The blinders were removed, and I understood that God never abandoned me; He held me close to Him. I had been razed, but God was rebuilding me upon the foundation of His love.

With my eyes wide open I could see how valuable I was to God. I felt the warmth of His touch in intimate worship. I could hear His voice whispering in my ear, comforting me. Let me tell you, His love is better than life itself. Surely the Lord was with me, and I knew it not. Everything I needed was there all along in God. It took me being between a rock and a hard place to understand that in my weakness God is made strong. His love is satisfying and leaves you wanting for nothing.

Patti LaBelle's 1978 song "You Are My Friend" perfectly expresses the kind of friend God revealed Himself to be during my wilderness experience.

You are my friend,
I never knew it 'til then
My friend, my friend
You hold my hand,
You might not say a word
But I see your tears when I show my pain
You're—my, my friend
I never knew it 'til then
My friend
I feel your love,
When you're not near
It helps me make it knowing you care
The thought of you helps me carry on
When I feel all hope is gone
I see the world with brand-new eyes
Your love has made me realize
My future looks bright to me,
Oh because you are my friend
I've been looking around and you were here all the time.[1]

Upon waking from his glorious dream, Jacob memorialized his experience by using the stone upon which he slept as the foundation of a pillar he built to honor God (Gen. 28:18). He called that place Bethel, which means a sacred place or sanctuary. When we wake up, we must mark the place where God made Himself known to us, the place where God spoke life to our dead situation. After you awaken, your wilderness season becomes your place of testimony. It becomes the place where you can draw strength for yourself and others.

Before I was positioned between a rock and a hard place, another pastor's wife desperately sought my help because her husband committed adultery. She called me, but I had no clue how to effectively minister to her. I prayed a prayer that had no real authority in the Spirit, and I ended the conversation by saying, "If you need me, call me." I am sure she said to herself, "What for?" Unfortunately she left the conversation feeling no different.

But *now* I know how to effectively minister to those who are grieving and are between a rock and a hard place. I have new authority in the Spirit because I know that I know that I know God is more than able to do exceedingly and abundantly more than we can ever ask or even think. It was at the Rock where God told me that my latter would be greater, better, and more joyous than my former. I thank God for my wilderness experience. It gave me strength and stability in Christ. It has become a blessed place where God showed me that He dwells above my problems.

THE ROCK WILL CHANGE YOUR NAME

Jacob was left alone. He had experienced Bethel and gained strength from the Word of God. Jacob knew his future was not bleak. He understood that even though he was in a bad situation with his brother wanting to kill him, God was on his side. Jacob had a newfound confidence, but he was not finished with the wilderness. Years later, after he married and had children, Jacob again found himself alone in the wilderness and between a rock and a hard place.

God had instructed Jacob to return to the land of his fathers and his family (Gen. 32). That meant meeting his brother, Esau, for the first since Jacob stole his birthright. Jacob was understandably nervous about the reunion. He feared Esau might attack him and attempt to kill his wives and children. This time in the wilderness Jacob was forced to face himself.

Jacob was used to making his own way in life, deceiving people when necessary. He had a history of relying on his own strength. But alone in the wilderness Jacob had to deal with the person he had become. When the glory of God was revealed to the prophet Isaiah, he felt undone and called himself a man of unclean lips (Isa. 6:1–5). The closer Jacob got to God, the more he saw his conniving and deceitful ways. And the more he saw himself, the more obvious his deficiencies became. When we are between a rock and a hard place, we have no choice but to face our situations and ourselves.

When I was in the wilderness, I came to terms with who I had become, and I began to see myself without all the hats I had been wearing. Not the wife, mother, daughter, pastor, or business owner—I had to look at *me*. I had allowed myself to walk in fear because I was so concerned with other people's opinions. Filled with doubt and disbelief, I had allowed myself to live well short of the full life in Christ that was available to me. I had stopped developing myself and instead became like a chandelier, simply a fixture in the house. Rather than refusing the rejection of my husband, I accepted it. Taking an honest look at myself was as heartbreaking for me as I am sure it was for Jacob.

After he sent his family to safety, Jacob encountered a man with whom he wrestled until the breaking of day (Gen. 32:24). This was no ordinary confrontation. The fight didn't end in a few minutes. It was exhausting and stressful. Jacob was in hand-to-hand combat and didn't know if he was going to live or die.

Yet Jacob persisted. The Bible says he wrestled with the man all night and refused to let go until he was blessed. As a result of his persistence God changed his name from Jacob, which meant deceitful, to Israel, which means "for as a prince hast thou power with God and with men, and hast prevailed" (Gen. 32:28, KJV). What an awesome testament to the power in a name and how a person's nature can be changed if he will examine himself.

When I was in the wilderness, I had to ask myself how I became this unhappy person. Why did I allow myself to be devalued and disrespected when I knew God considered me royalty? How did I allow ministry to become drudgery instead of a privilege? I wanted to be changed. No longer did I want my name to describe hurt, pain, sadness, or fear. I desperately needed a new name. Between a rock and a hard place, where nobody was available to help me, God changed my name. "Defeated" and "hopeless" no longer described me. I walked in victory, power, wholeness, peace, and satisfaction.

THE ROCK WILL GRANT PROVISION

In Exodus 17 Moses encountered a rather "rocky" situation. Having led the children of Israel out of Egypt, Moses and his followers came upon a place called Rephidim, where there was no water for anyone to drink (Exod. 17:1). The people grew angry with Moses and demanded that he give them water. Fearing he would be stoned if he did not comply, Moses cried out to God for guidance. God told Moses to take his staff and strike the rock in Horeb, and water would flow from it. Moses obeyed, and their thirst was quenched.

Here is an awesome testimony of God's power. The children of Israel were tired and hungry in the wilderness. It hadn't been that long since God parted the Red Sea to usher them past their Egyptian pursuers, but they hadn't entered the Promised Land yet. The Israelites were in their wilderness, literally and spiritually. They were between a rock and a hard place.

That place was so difficult to bear, the Israelites began to long for the familiarity of Egypt despite having endured four hundred years of slavery. Ahead of them was uncharted territory, an uncertain future. The feelings of insecurity became so great the Israelites almost stoned Moses. And when Moses sought God for help, the Lord told him to go hit a rock with a stick.

Isn't that the way our God is? We pray for a specific remedy, only to receive a seemingly illogical answer. God's ways are not our own. Naaman, captain of the Syrian army, went to Elisha the prophet to be healed of leprosy. When Naaman arrived, Elisha sent a messenger to tell Naaman to dip seven times in the Jordan River (2 Kings 5:9–10).

Now the waters of the Jordan were notoriously unpleasant. Naaman saw no correlation between bathing in those waters and being clean, much less being cured of leprosy. He almost missed his blessing because he felt his solution didn't fit his situation. Naaman was stuck between a rock and a hard place; outside of God nothing could save him. So he put aside his pride and dipped seven times. When he arose from the murky waters after the seventh dip, he was free from leprosy.

How many times have we refused God's blessings because they were not packaged the way we had envisioned? God answers us in the midst of our most dire needs, yet we run the risk of missing His provision if we're looking for it to arrive a certain way.

You may want to leave your hometown for the Big Apple, but God instructs you to head for the South. Why would God tell you to venture south when you wanted so badly to go north? Don't disregard God's seemingly illogical instruction. When God gives an instruction that makes no sense, He is planting a seed that can be nurtured and harvested only through faith.

Only through faith will you see God's hand of provision. Allow God to orchestrate divine appointments and connections to further His call on your life. Let God be sovereign in your life, and trust His answers to your problems. Obedience is better than sacrifice (1 Sam. 15).

Moses needed water for himself and the people, and God told him to strike the rock. Now *that's* illogical. It did not make a bit of sense. Yet it was the answer that brought forth provision. It was at the rock that God brought supernatural sustenance to Moses and the Israelites, and the Rock will also supernaturally provide for you.

I can attest to this. After my husband's infidelity was exposed, several employees of the church decided to leave. As a result they had no income. Of course I felt somewhat responsible for their situation, and my heart broke for them. I found myself sowing into their lives monthly until they could find jobs. I also gave lump sums to others to assist them until they obtained health insurance. I sowed out of my need. This was a huge sacrifice because I was not yet divorced, so I was not receiving child support or alimony. At that point I was living off a portion of what was in our bank account.

After I started a church of my own, Majestic Life Ministries, I did not take a salary for the first two years. I instead persistently worked my network marketing business in order to generate income for my family. It was extremely challenging for me to devote the necessary time to both endeavors. But I believe God was teaching me to trust Him, and He was developing in me a pure heart toward ministry. I never saw the ministry as a paycheck, but after my experience in the wilderness, I can truly say I minister because I love God and His people and for no other reason.

THE ROCK EMPOWERS YOU TO WAR IN THE SPIRIT

Rizpah is one of my favorite personalities in the Bible. She had a tenacious fight that just would not quit. Soon after David became king, drought struck the land, causing a famine. When David inquired of the Lord, God told him there was drought because Saul tried to annihilate the Gibeonites after the Israelites had sworn to spare them. To atone for this sin David handed seven descendants of Saul over to the Gibeonites, including Rizpah's two sons. The Gibeonites killed the seven men and put their bodies on public display as a sign of victory.

Typically such corpses met further shame and desecration by serving as food sources for carrion animals. But Rizpah wouldn't have it. The Bible says after her sons were killed, Rizpah spread her sackcloth upon a rock and remained there until the drought ended. Theologians believe Rizpah's vigil lasted several weeks if not months. What was Rizpah doing upon the rock? She did not want her sons' bodies to be defiled by wild animals, so she alone stood between her children and the predators lurking in the wilderness.

Let's look at this a little deeper. I remember one day leaving home to make an appointment. In my peripheral vision I saw what appeared to be a small dog by the trash can sitting at the curb for pickup. I looked a little closer and noticed that the dog was oddly shaped. When I approached the animal, it was no dog at all; it was a vulture. I attempted to chase the bird away. But that big, ugly bird had the nerve to stare me down as if to say, "What do you think *you're* gonna do?"

Imagine huge vultures trying to eat Rizpah's sons hanging on a tree. I'm sure she faced injury from their huge beaks and sharp talons. Yet she stayed put for several agonizing weeks. That was Rizpah's only job. At night there were wolves, lions, and other nocturnal beasts looking for food. She had to brave the cold, dark, dangerous uncertainty of the night alone. The Bible says she succeeded in keeping her sons' bodies safe from the birds by day and the beast of the field by night.

At the rock Rizpah battled for her children, and when we're between a rock and a hard place, we learn how to do spiritual warfare. I know of couples whose children have decided to live an alternative lifestyle, fallen into drug addiction, or become promiscuous. The parents did not throw their children away; instead they made a decision to cover their children in love and wage war against the evil spirits that sought to overtake them.

Rizpah did not have anyone to help her in the natural realm. She was alone in the darkness of night; yet, supernaturally, she stood. The warfare season will last longer than one prayer; it may last longer than one year. My wilderness season lasted almost three years. I felt that I was literally in a fight for my life because depression wanted to devour me; I knew giving up was not an option.

Rizpah stood on the rock to fight off everything that would come to devour her children. In a similar way we must stand on the Rock to gain the strength to fight the enemy's attempts to devour our hope and the dreams God has given us for our future.

The Bible says a servant told David what Rizpah was doing. It so moved his heart that he took her sons' bones and gave them a proper burial, restoring to some degree the honor and dignity that had been lost. When we take a stand to fight for what is ours—whether it's our children, marriage, or ministry—God will take notice, and He will bless us. Don't give up. We must press onward and fight the good fight of faith.

So again, is anybody out there with you when you're in between a rock and a hard place? The answer is no; there is no "body" out there. There is no human being who can help you. But when you cry out to God for help, you begin to walk down the path He has cleared for you. It is OK to be between a rock and a hard place when you run to the Rock.

I can gain strength from the Rock, because He is the one who gives me hope as my purpose and destiny are revealed. The Rock is where my name is changed from something weak to something powerful. The Rock is where I receive provision for my journey. And the Rock empowers me to war against the enemy. The hard place pales in comparison to the Rock. As long as I am touching the Rock, that in-between place is not so hard. God's grace softens our difficult journey. As Romans 8:31 says, "If God be for us, who can be against us?" (KJV).

TAKE A
LOOK INSIDE

People spend a fortune on health and beauty products. Even in a down economy, men and women alike find ways to ensure they look their best. But the Lord has never been particularly impressed with our outer appearance or status. In Matthew 23:27, Jesus said, "Woe unto you, scribes and Pharisees, hypocrites! For ye are like unto whited sepulchres, which indeed appear beautiful outward, but are within full of dead men's bones, and of all uncleanness" (KJV).

The New International Version says it another way: "Woe to you, teachers of the law and Pharisees, you hypocrites! You are like white-washed tombs, which look beautiful on the outside but on the inside are full of dead men's bones and everything unclean." Jesus scolded the religious elite for putting up façades of righteousness that belied the uncleanness in their private lives. We constantly see in Scripture that God values a person's character over his appearance. Therefore, in order to examine the true measure of a Christian, we must take a look inside.

Many years ago when I was living in Baltimore, Maryland, I partici-pated in a women's ministry led by the first lady of the church I attended. For a particular lesson she was teaching, the first lady instructed all the women to decorate a plain box with anything that described who they were. If a person liked to cook, then she could adorn her box with pictures or items related to cooking. If a person liked music, cosmetology, children, or the outdoors, the box was to be decorated accordingly.

The day our boxes were due, there were quite a few elaborate offerings. Many of the boxes were painstakingly decorated and quite beautiful. There were huge boxes, small boxes, sparkling boxes, and plush boxes. The broad spectrum of colors and designs provided an amazing insight into the personalities and interests of the women at the church.

After every box was submitted, we found out our assignment was not complete. The first lady then instructed us to decorate the inside of the box to express our most painful experiences. The room became somber as the meeting adjourned. For most of us, this task was extremely challenging. In order for us to decorate the inside of the box, we had to examine the inside of ourselves.

Many of us had buried our painful experiences, never wanting to relive them. We would have to dig into the cracks and crevices of our souls and touch the pain of yesterday. The assignment was only made more difficult by the fact that we would actually have to figure out which items best represented our greatest pain so we could use them to decorate the inside of our boxes.

The ladies gathered once more to display their boxes. There was a lot less laughter during this meeting; the atmosphere was much more subdued. This time, as each woman's box was inspected, something supernatural took place. In presenting and explaining the inside of our boxes, we opened ourselves up to the women around us, and as a result we learned a great deal about ourselves.

Some of the women realized they were still holding on to unforgiveness, and because they had not been healed of past hurts, they were sabotaging new relationships. In other cases women discovered they had been living in a self-protective mode, not realizing they had imprisoned the vibrant women God made them to be. We began to authentically "see" one another. We began to better understand one another—what made us tick or why we behaved the way we did. We were also able to see the supernatural strength to overcome that God put inside us.

When we examined the outside of the box, we gained no real insight. The exterior masked the complexities within. It was not until we examined the inside of the box that we began to see one another for who we truly were. A shiny, red apple can look delicious from the outside, but you have to cut into it to see whether a worm is lurking inside.

Inside is defined as the inner or interior part; the inward character, perceptions or feelings; the middle part; inner organs; or secret information.[1] This chapter is going to challenge you to truly take a look inside.

MISPLACED CONFIDENCE

In Matthew 26, Jesus was sitting with His disciples, sharing the Passover meal. The disciples sat beside Jesus with heavy hearts, knowing He would soon be leaving them. The disciples cherished every moment they had with their Master. But as He sat with them sharing the last supper they would have together, Jesus revealed something that amplified their grief. As they were eating, He said, "Assuredly, I say to you, one of you will betray Me" (v. 21, NKJV).

The disciples were completely baffled, and each began to ask Him, "Lord, is it I?" Each looked within to see if he was capable of betraying Jesus, the Man whom they worshiped and greatly loved. When his turn came, Judas responded, "Surely not I, Rabbi?" (v. 25). The disciples who loved Christ dearly were humble enough to examine themselves. Yet Judas, the very one who betrayed Jesus, responded with self-assurance.

Many make the mistake of being overly confident in their own goodness. Peter was such a man, extremely confident that he knew himself. He told Jesus, "Even if all are made to stumble because of you, I will never be made to stumble....Even if I have to die with You, I will not deny You" (Matt. 26:33, 35, NKJV). Well, we all know how that story ended. When confronted by a suspicious servant girl, Peter denied that he knew Jesus. In fact, he denied Him three times in a matter of hours.

That night Peter learned and taught us all a great lesson—that confidence in oneself is misplaced. Our confidence can only be in Christ, who is our righteousness. We must understand that only by God's grace can we live successfully. We are nothing without His Spirit. "So, if you think you are standing firm, be careful that you don't fall!" (1 Cor. 10:12).

I made the huge mistake of trusting myself more than I should have. I never exuded an overabundance of confidence, nor was I an extrovert. I definitely did not consider myself an expert in any area, and I did not think I was better than anyone else. Looking at my quiet, unassuming temperament, most people would never have realized that I trusted myself. I didn't know it myself.

I had a great testimony. I had been in church all my life, never gave my parents much trouble, never drank or smoked, never went to any raucous college parties, and I saved myself for the man I married. My life was pretty drama free. I did my best to stay in the will and protection of the Almighty. Even though I sincerely loved people and walked humbly before others, I somehow thought I was immune to "their" problems. I subconsciously believed certain things only happened to "other" people.

Proverbs 3:5 says, "Trust in the LORD with all you heart, and lean not on your own understanding." I thought I had life figured out. One plus one has to equal two, right? That may be true in the natural, but it is not necessarily so in the spirit realm. God's ways defy finite logic. Americans are raised believing that if we earn good grades in school, we will be able to attend a good college, get a good job, and make a good salary. That logic no longer holds true because our country is experiencing spiritual judgment from God in the form of an economic downturn.

I believed if you lived a holy life, you would never have the painful experiences of those who did not submit to God's ways. I came to the realization that my understanding was absolutely wrong, and I had to trust God for the spiritual revelation of my life. I had a very hard time comprehending the fact that I was experiencing the pain and betrayal I thought only "other" people encountered. The Bible says, "The good man brings good things out of the good stored up in him, and the evil man brings evil things out of the evil stored up in him" (Matt. 12:35). So what did I do wrong to have so much evil in my life? I was completely clueless.

When diagnosing a problem with a car, most people look under the hood. We should do the same thing when something goes wrong in our lives. We must check under our hoods and take a look inside. When I did this, I embarked on a revealing journey that showed me exactly what was going on inside my spirit, soul, and body.

I would often pray through Psalm 139. In this chapter the psalmist is speaking to God about all of his enemies, who are surrounding him. He makes his situation seem virtually hopeless. Yet as he cried out to the Lord, he gave Him all the praise and acknowledged God's sovereignty. That chapter ends with the psalmist saying, "Search me, O God, and know my heart; test me and know my anxious thoughts. See if there is any offensive way in me, and lead me in the way everlasting" (Ps. 139:23–24). This is a pure scripture to pray if you really want God to answer your prayers.

When I looked under my hood, so to speak, God began to show me things I did not like. I saw that I had become self-righteous. It was not because of any goodness of my own that I lived a righteous life, but it was by the grace of God that I was obedient to the Scriptures. Yes, I made the choice to live holy before God, but that did not give me the right to look down on others if they missed the mark.

If not careful, I could have become like the Pharisees. I could have failed to operate in *rhema*, or the spirit of the Word, and lost compassion for those who had made devastating mistakes in life. Thank God He showed me myself. The scales began to fall from my eyes as I thought of different people who had fallen or were going through trials similar to mine, and my heart broke for them. I felt an overwhelming love toward them. This was also the beginning of my breakthrough with my husband. I began to feel sorry for him and wanted him to be healed. I wanted him to be whole again, and I no longer felt such intense anger toward him.

My twin sister, Rená, experienced something similar when she asked God to search her heart. Rená is administratively astute. She majored in political science in college and began her career in Washington DC, working for the federal government. Like my mother, Rita, my sister was quickly promoted through the ranks. Both she and my mother held prestigious professional positions and enjoyed wonderful opportunities to travel overseas.

Because she was a perfectionist, Rená often took on more than was necessary. She found herself obsessed with doing for others. But what concerned her was she also wanted to be acknowledged for her actions even though she often volunteered herself. She began to pray that the Lord would reveal what was going on in her heart. She wasn't expecting Him to answer the way He did.

God began to show my sister that there was some emotional hurt in her heart and flaws in her ways. The process God took her through was detailed and excruciatingly painful for Rená. God began to literally gut areas of her life that Rená thought were perfect. She found herself crying for days on end. But Rená allowed God to examine her heart under His microscope and then perform surgery. Rená described the experience as gut-wrenching, but because she allowed the Lord to have His way, she experienced more freedom and an increase in spiritual authority.

GOD KNOWS EVERYTHING

The psalmist said, "O LORD, you have searched me and you know me. You know when I sit and when I rise; you perceive my thoughts from afar. You discern my going out and my lying down; you are familiar with all my ways. Before a word is on my tongue you know it completely" (Ps. 139:1–4). We can't tell God anything He does not already know. He knows us better than we know ourselves. He has numbered the very hairs on our head, and He knows our thoughts before we think them. He is totally aware of what is lurking in our hearts, even when we aren't willing to admit it to ourselves or to others. He is the master, and we must inquire of Him for answers to the things we don't understand.

"You have searched me and you know me." The word *searched* means "to examine thoroughly."[2] God can perceive your thoughts from afar (v. 2). He sees and knows the interior of your mind. He knows the thoughts

you never express, the ones that never see the light of day. God knows the words you will say before you say them (v. 4).

The Word says in Jeremiah 17:9 that the heart is deceitful above all things. You may think you know yourself, but you very well may be deceived. You need the Holy Spirit to show you what is really there. That is why the psalmist's prayer in Psalm 139:23—"Search me, O God, and know my heart"—is one of the wisest prayers you can pray. We all need God's help to see inside our hearts. God is intimately acquainted with *all* our ways (v. 3). He knows not only what we do but also how we do it, not only where we go but also how we get there, not only who we know but also how we know them, not only what we say but also how we say it. The Lord knows:

 Our location. In John 1:47 Jesus identified Nathanael as "a true Israelite, in whom there is nothing false." Nathanael understandably asked Jesus how He could possibly know that. Jesus said, "I saw you while you were still under the fig tree" (v. 48). Nathanael was amazed by Jesus's knowledge of him—so much so that he responded by declaring, "Rabbi, you are the Son of God; you are the King of Israel" (v. 49).

- *Our ways.* Jesus knew Nicodemus was living in frustration, as his religious activities were bringing him no peace. His ways were hidden from himself but not from God. This is why Jesus talked to him about a new birth—a completely new approach to God (John 3:1–20).

- *Our thoughts.* Before Zacchaeus ever uttered a word, Jesus knew the man's thoughts, specifically that he was tired of the wicked life he had been living and was ready to repent. When Zacchaeus did speak after Jesus arrived at his house, he proclaimed, "Look, Lord! Here and now I give half of my possessions to the poor, and if I have cheated anybody

out of anything, I will pay back four times the amount"
(Luke 19:8). Jesus saw that he was truly repentant and told
him, "Today salvation has come to this house" (v. 9).

- *Our secrets.* When Jesus stopped at the well in Samaria,
  He encountered a woman and asked her for a drink of
  water. It was there that He famously said, "Whoever
  drinks the water I give him will never thirst. Indeed, the
  water I give him will become in him a spring of water
  welling up to eternal life" (John 4:14).

  When the Samaritan woman asked Jesus for the water
  He was offering, He told her to go, call her husband, and
  return (v. 16). She evasively replied that she had no husband, to which Jesus responded, "You are right when you
  say you have no husband. The fact is, you have had five
  husbands, and the man you now have is not your husband.
  What you have just said is quite true" (vv. 17–18). Jesus
  knew the truth behind the woman's words because He
  knew her fully—what she was revealing and what she was
  hiding.

When I went to God asking Him to show me myself, I sincerely
thought I would receive great news. I rehearsed in my mind how obedient I had been throughout my life. What I was going through made
me the perfect martyr. My attitude was a lot like that of the rich young
ruler, who came to Jesus asking what he must do to inherit eternal life.
Jesus told him to keep the commandments, and the man replied that he
had kept them since he was a child. But instead of applauding this young
ruler, the Lord proceeded to reveal what was truly in the man's heart.

> When Jesus heard this, he said to him, "You still lack one thing.
> Sell everything you have and give to the poor, and you will have
> treasure in heaven. Then come, follow me." When he heard this, he
> became very sad, because he was a man of great wealth.
>
> —LUKE 18:22–23

Just like the rich young ruler, I thought God was going to praise me for the life I had lived and condemn everyone who betrayed me. I felt my commitment to God had been impeccable. I had attended Christian schools since the fifth grade, and in college I did not stray from my walk with Him. I was a good wife and mother. I was, however, in for a very rude awakening. God revealed my heart to me, and I was not pleased.

BURIED TALENTS

As the Holy Spirit began to show me what was truly in my heart, He took me to the parable of the talents in Matthew 25. In the parable a man entrusts his wealth to three servants. To one he gave five talents, to another two, and to another one, each according to his ability. He went away on a trip, and when he returned, he inquired of the servants to see what happened to his wealth. The servant who had received five talents put them to work and had earned ten; the servant with two talents gained two more. But the man who had one talent wasn't much of an overachiever.

> Then the man who had received the one talent came. "Master," he said, "I knew that you are a hard man, harvesting where you have not sown and gathering where you have not scattered seed. So I was afraid and went out and hid your talent in the ground. See, here is what belongs to you."
>
> His master replied, "You wicked, lazy servant! So you knew that I harvest where I have not sown and gather where I have not scattered seed? Well then, you should have put my money on deposit with the bankers, so that when I returned I would have received it back with interest. Take the talent from him and give it to the one who has the ten talents. For everyone who has will be given more, and he will have an abundance. Whoever does not have, even what he has will be taken from him. And throw that worthless servant outside, into the darkness, where there will be weeping and gnashing of teeth."
>
> —MATTHEW 25:24–30

God showed me that I buried my gifts and anointing because of fear. God had called me to "see" prophetically and help keep spiritual order in the house. I remember times when He beckoned me to speak up; He instructed me to step out and would call me to prophesy. But if my husband opposed my moving forward, I would acquiesce and call it humility. Yet God called it fear! I realize now that if had I been in position, my husband would have been held to a higher level of accountability, and things may have been different in our marriage. I had to take ownership and responsibility for my contribution to the problems that surfaced in our home.

The irony is that God still required me to do everything He previously called me to do. When God gives us an assignment and our circumstances change before it is completed, we are still required to finish the task. Just look at Jonah. He tried to run from what God called him to do, but God allowed a storm to come and a great fish to swallow Jonah. When God commanded the fish to vomit Jonah out on dry land, He again told him to go preach to Nineveh. And that time Jonah obeyed.

Like Jonah I could run, but I couldn't hide. God again positioned me to preach, prophesy, and lead a church. This time the fear was even stronger, and I did not want to do it, but I learned to truly trust God. As Proverbs 29:25 says, "Fear of man will prove to be a snare, but whoever trusts in the LORD is kept safe." I was reminded that God knew me before I was conceived, and He gave me an assignment and purpose that must be completed. When each of us stands before the Lord, it won't matter if our best friend, parents, or spouse fulfilled the calling God gave them. We will all be held accountable for our actions.

I didn't know how this could be. God was calling me to pastor *again*? I didn't want to lead a church anymore. I pleaded with God, "Is there any other way?" I cried every day hoping God would change His mind. What would everyone say? In time I came to see the only thing that mattered was what God and His Word said. I had to lean on scriptures such as Hebrews 13:6, "So we say with confidence, 'The Lord is my helper; I will not be afraid. What can man do to me?'" Or, "Do not be afraid of those who kill the body but cannot kill the soul. Rather, be afraid of the One who can destroy both soul and body in hell" (Matt. 10:28).

I was able to push past the fear and pursue God's calling on my life, because I realized that God has covered and protected me. Had I passed the test the first time, I would not have had to take it again. Fear often tries to grip me, because the road ahead is challenging, especially as a single mom. This is not the road I would have chosen, but the Lord has proven to be my battle-axe, and I give Him all the glory.

INEFFECTIVE MINISTRY

Jesus was passing through a village and stopped to visit friends. A woman named Martha opened her home to Him and was busy making preparations for her guests while her sister Mary sat at the Lord's feet listening to everything He had to say. Martha complained to Jesus that she was doing all the work. But instead of sympathizing with Martha, He gently corrected her.

> "Martha, Martha," the Lord answered, "you are worried and upset about many things, but only one thing is needed. Mary has chosen what is better, and it will not be taken away from her."
>
> —LUKE 10:41–42

I can relate to both Mary and Martha. During the last few years my husband and I were married, ministry started to become drudgery to me, and I did not realize how weary I was. I lived in perpetual denial. I remember speaking to another female co-pastor, and she seemed bewildered by my disposition toward ministry. She said ministry had its challenges, but it should mostly be fun and enjoyable. That stuck with me because I remembered a time when it used to be enjoyable.

Many first ladies and female co-pastors have to deal with people in their churches who don't want them to succeed in ministry. They have to contend with leaders and members alike who try to position themselves between the pastor and his wife. I grew so tired of fighting individuals who wanted to take my leadership role in the church that I eventually stopped pushing back. I wanted nothing to do with people who wanted only to impress my husband and had no regard for the conviction and leading of the Holy Spirit. So I didn't fight as hard, and before long I was no longer fully walking in my assignment.

My national women's conference notwithstanding, I became ineffective in ministry. I turned into the trophy wife I always said I would never be. Although I sincerely cared about the members and continued to serve them, I did not have the zeal I once possessed. I didn't choose the better way Mary chose. I didn't sit at the feet of Jesus. I didn't allow my spirit to gain strength by worshiping the Lord. I didn't keep Jesus's agenda before my husband's agenda or even my own. I lost my sense of purpose and identity in the work of ministry rather than in the God of the ministry. I needed Jesus to take me aside and remind me, "Only one thing is needed." That one thing is Him.

HIDDEN SIN

I viewed myself as sinless and thought those who committed sin just didn't want to live right. As a result I was very judgmental, but I didn't know it. I hadn't learned the truth found in the Book of James.

> Blessed is the man who perseveres under trial, because when he has stood the test, he will receive the crown of life that God has promised to those who love him. When tempted, no one should say, "God is tempting me." For God cannot be tempted by evil, nor does he tempt anyone; but each one is tempted when, by his own evil desire, he is dragged away and enticed. Then, after desire has conceived, it gives birth to sin; and sin, when it is full-grown, gives birth to death.
>
> —JAMES 1:12–15

When my husband was being unfaithful, there was a tremendous amount of warfare in our home. Our children were seeing demons and images of large spiders and unidentifiable bugs projecting through the walls and ceilings. Occasionally I saw a demonic figure in the shape of a woman with a black cloak covering her face climbing the stairs of our home. Our yard was filled with black snakes, and a live snake actually manifested in our home. There was a heaviness in our home that was almost tangible. Sin had given the enemy access.

A member of my church wrote a book titled *Through the Eyes of a Nobody*. It deals with the transfer of spirits through sexual intercourse. A spiritual soul tie is formed with every sex partner a person has. Accordingly people open themselves to the spirits operating in those with whom they have intercourse. My husband brought the spirits he received through infidelity back home to me. And it influenced the church because whatever is on the head of the church goes down to the lay members. Marriages in our church were in trouble, teens were getting pregnant, and singles were struggling to abstain from sexual activity.

After I learned of my husband's infidelity, I found myself becoming obsessed with sex. I wanted to understand why he cheated. What wasn't I doing? I read books, surfed the Internet, and even visited porn sites to get a better understanding of what I must have been lacking. Little did I know, I was being influenced by a spirit of perversion that had entered my marriage as a result of my husband's unfaithfulness.

I didn't realize that by focusing so much on sex I was allowing lust to permeate my spirit. I remember thinking I should get a boyfriend to experience intimacy with someone else, and I really didn't see anything wrong with the idea. My spirit had become weak, and I had somehow convinced myself that being with someone else would make me feel better. Thank God for family and accountability sisters who were watching every step I made.

I remember going to the beach with my sister and my mom just to get away for a while. We were at a restaurant, and our blond-haired, blue-eyed waiter was very attentive. When we were about to leave, he turned to me and asked if he could get my phone number and take me out. Without hesitation I said, "Yes!" I gave him my number, and he walked away. When I looked at my mom and sister sitting across from me, their mouths hung open, and their eyes were bulging. They were shocked. Later on I was shocked too. The spirit of rejection had me thinking no one would ever want me. But when I came to my senses, I was so scared the waiter would actually call me that I changed my phone number!

So why am I sharing this with you? I want you to see that when your spirit is weak, sin can and will bring chaos into your life. Instead of resisting temptation, you will be drawn away by the lust hidden inside you. If you do not have the mind of Christ, it is easy to fall. As the Lord began to show me myself, I began to have compassion for my husband. I realized that he allowed his spirit to become weak and over time became dull to the Holy Spirit.

I thank God I had what I call my "Chastity Belt Posse," which consisted of my sister, a group of intercessors, and some close friends. They basically smothered me and watched every move I made to ensure I would not fall into sexual sin. In my weakened state I allowed myself to occasionally engage in inappropriate phone conversations. I would always confess to God and to the "Chastity Belt Posse." That was my way of staying accountable.

If they could have, I am *sure* my posse would have been with me twenty-four hours a day. Of course they couldn't. God's grace kept me. But I don't like to think about what might have happened if I didn't have people to hold me accountable. I had a desire to sin. Jesus taught that "anyone who looks at a woman lustfully has already committed adultery with her in his heart" (Matt. 5:28). Sin begins in the heart.

Throughout this chapter we have been talking about our hearts. That is what God is most concerned with. He wants the attitude of our hearts to be right before Him. Even though my thoughts had not manifested into actions, I was still guilty of disappointing God because my heart was filthy. It wasn't obvious from the outside, but when I took a look inside, I could see how much I hurt my Lord.

I was not aware that I had lust, hatred, fear, and doubt hidden within me until God revealed it. The Bible talks about silly women. Second Timothy 3:6 says, "They are the kind who worm their way into homes and gain control over weak-willed women, who are loaded down with sins and are swayed by all kinds of evil desires." *Ouch!* I thank God for loving me enough to expose and correct me. The Bible tells us that the Lord chastens those He loves.

> "Do not make light of the Lord's discipline, and do not lose heart when he rebukes you because the Lord disciplines those he loves, and he punishes everyone he accepts as a son." Endure hardship as discipline; God is treating you as sons. For what son is not disciplined by his father? If you are not disciplined (and everyone undergoes discipline), then you are illegitimate children and not true sons.
>
> —HEBREWS 12:5–8

I desired to be accepted and not rejected, but I did not realize what was truly going on in my heart. It wasn't until God revealed the condition of my heart that I became accountable to others and focused on doing what was right. James 4:17 says, "Anyone, then, who knows the good he ought to do and doesn't do it, sins."

After God showed me the sin I had fallen into—and the sin I almost fell into—God began holding me accountable to keep my heart free of lust, fear, doubt, and so forth. The process was difficult, but it was the least I could do. I asked God to create in me a clean heart. I didn't want Him to refurbish the one I already had. I wanted God to get rid of it and give me a heart that was completely new.

CHAPTER
6

FREEDOM THROUGH FORGIVENESS

It is easy to say we have forgiven someone but much more difficult to truly release all bitterness toward those who have wronged us. That is because true forgiveness is more than lip service; it is a matter of the heart. And it is possible for our hearts to be sick with unforgiveness without our even knowing it.

The Bible tells us, "The spiritual did not come first, but the natural, and after that the spiritual.... And just as we have borne the likeness of the earthly man, so shall we bear the likeness of the man from heaven" (1 Cor. 15:46, 49). In order to understand the importance of having a heart of forgiveness, we must first explore our natural heart.

By the twenty-fifth day of a woman's pregnancy, the baby's heart has formed and is pumping blood. Some doctors say death actually occurs when the heart stops beating because the heart develops and is "alive" before the brain and continues beating after the brain has died.[1] It is in the heart where our lives begin, and in the same way it is in the spiritual heart where our spiritual lives begin.

With each beat of that unborn baby's heart, the mother and child begin to bond. She doesn't wait until the baby is born to connect with the child. During the gestational period mothers prophesy over their babies. We give our children names and eat nutritious food so they will be properly nourished. We prepare the nursery, and if we can afford it, buy more clothes than any child could ever wear. And all of this happens before the child is born.

The same holds true in the Spirit. Before we were in our mother's womb, our spiritual heart was beating and God knew us. The Bible says, "Before I formed you in the womb I knew you, before you were born I set you apart; I appointed you as a prophet to the nations" (Jer. 1:4–5). The "knowing" referred to in this verse points to an intimate connection. God knew us intimately. He intimately knew our purpose, personality, future, and heart.

God spoke our destinies and prepared our lives before we came into the earth. Romans 8:29 says, "For those God foreknew he also predestined to be conformed to the likeness of his Son, that he might be the firstborn among many brothers." Nothing that happens in our lives ever comes as a surprise to God.

He knew our spouses would cheat on us or that our loved one would die unexpectedly. He knew all the tragedies that would befall us. But He has also promised to never leave us. We must understand that we cannot change what has happened to us, but we can change who we become as a result of those tragedies by deciding whether to forgive.

When our children are born, they seem innocent and sweet. But we're all born with a sin nature. Because of that predisposition to sin, our hearts gravitate toward revenge instead of forgiveness, hate instead of love, hurt instead of joy. What comes naturally is a tendency to hold grudges and a desire for the offender to hurt just as much as or more than we do.

Americans crave instant gratification; when we are wronged, we want "instant revenge." You may have seen incidences of road rage and heard about revenge killings; in both situations a perceived offense is met with instant, violent retaliation. Instead of forgiving the wrongdoer, we take matters into our own hands, becoming vigilantes, even though God says, "It is mine to avenge; I will repay" (Rom. 12:19).

Man's revenge pales in comparison to God's. When the Creator of all things has promised to exact revenge for us, the only thing that can be keeping us from extending forgiveness is pride. If we are humbly submitted to the Holy Spirit, forgiveness, not revenge, should be our natural response to offense. This is a struggle, I know, but forgiveness must win. I'll explain why.

The Bible says, "The heart is deceitful above all things, and desperately wicked; who can know it? I, the LORD, search the heart, I test the mind, even to give every man according to his ways" (Jer. 17:9–10, NKJV). The heart is deceitful, and as we discussed in the last chapter, it is hard to truly know what is inside of it. Many in the body of Christ are in danger of having a spiritual heart attack or a stroke and becoming spiritually disabled or, worse, spiritually dead because of unforgiveness.

People go into cardiac arrest every day completely unaware that they were at risk for such an attack. How could something that serious go unnoticed? Often there are no obvious warning signs. Even though they engage in unhealthy behavior, if there are no visible side effects, people won't realize the extent to which their arteries have become clogged or how much plaque has built up. If they can still function normally, why would they think something is wrong? Unfortunately the lack of outward signs does not guarantee the absence of inward turmoil, which is why we often don't find out about heart trouble until it's too late.

In the same way a spiritual heart can also be plagued with undetected disease. Saul is a perfect example. He became mighty in his own eyes, so God moved on and anointed someone else as king (1 Sam. 16). Sadly Saul didn't even realize his anointing was gone.

The heart has an ability to deceive itself. As a result it is possible to believe you have forgiven someone when in actuality, bitterness and unforgiveness are still festering. That was certainly happening to me. I sincerely thought I had forgiven those who hurt me, not realizing that forgiveness was a process I had not completed. I remember one day blurting out, "I hate him," completely out of the blue. I had no idea where those words came from or why they suddenly spilled out. The anger toward my husband had been inside of me undetected.

There would be more of those "I hate him" moments. My heart was still hurting, and though the pain was hidden for a while, eventually it began to manifest openly. Although I now felt sorry for my husband and I recognized my love for him, I was still imprisoned by unforgiveness.

In order to have true freedom in the spirit, I had to make the difficult decision to work on forgiving my husband. I had to humble myself and choose to speak kindly to him, encourage my children to show respect for him, pray for him, and not to speak negatively about him to those who thought the world of him. It was one of the most difficult things the Lord asked me to do, but it was also one of the most important.

There is a war raging within our members. Just as a natural heart will deteriorate if we keep eating greasy, fatty foods, so will the spiritual heart deteriorate if we feed it negative thoughts and feelings of unforgiveness. I made the decision to feed my heart positive thoughts about my husband, which starved unforgiveness and fed the love I still had for him.

FORGIVE AS YOU HAVE BEEN FORGIVEN

I've come to realize that quite a few people have amnesia. They have totally forgotten where they came from and how God delivered them. The same measure of grace that was extended to us should be the same measure of grace we extend to others.

I chuckle when I hear new moms and veteran mothers comparing their exhausting and painful labor experiences. Each woman tends to think hers was worse. I have four children, and each labor was excruciating, but I do not fully remember the pain I experienced. It's like the passage in John, "A woman giving birth to a child has pain because her time has come; but when her baby is born she forgets the anguish because of her joy that a child is born into the world" (John 16:21). Sometimes we can be so brash with people, thinking we know how they feel because we had a similar experience. But we may need to ask God to anoint us with compassion so we can truly understand what others are going through.

We may have the scars of the hurt but may not necessarily remember the pain we felt. We must evaluate the level of our compassion toward those in the middle of devastating trials.

Joyce Meyer once described being very sick during her fourth pregnancy. The situation confused her because she had been in good health during her previous pregnancies. When she asked God why she was so nauseous this time around, He took her to Matthew 7, which talks about judging others. Joyce said the Holy Spirit reminded her of a woman who used to attend her home Bible study. After the woman became pregnant, she often missed the Bible study because she was tired and ill.

Joyce used to criticize the young woman for not pressing through to attend the Bible study. She thought the woman just needed to toughen up. Now Joyce was in a similar situation—too sick to do much more than lie in bed. As soon as she repented of judging the woman, Joyce said her health was restored. She believes God allowed her to have that experience so she would learn to have greater compassion for others.[2]

Responding to hurtful experiences with love and forgiveness is often difficult, but as Christians we don't have an option. Jesus never hesitated to forgive, and He is our ultimate example.

I know many people wonder whether they must forgive someone who has not repented. I had to learn this the hard way, but you don't need the person's repentance to extend forgiveness. It's natural for us to want to hear the person who wronged us sincerely repent. I certainly wanted that. I thought that would be my sign that it was time to forgive. But God requires us to forgive even if the person who offended us never repents.

Just think of the thousands of rape victims and the families of murder victims who will never receive an apology. Are they to harbor hatred and bitterness the rest of their lives because they never heard the words "I'm sorry"? Absolutely not! They must forgive in order to be released from the prison of anger and resentment and experience true freedom.

"Then Peter came to Jesus and asked, 'Lord, how many times shall I forgive my brother when he sins against me? Up to seven times?' Jesus answered, 'I tell you, not seven times, but seventy-seven times'" (Matt. 18:21–22). Yikes! This is not a favorite verse for those who struggle with unforgiveness. While enduring the shame of crucifixion, Jesus said, "Father, forgive them; for they know not what they do" (Luke 23:34, KJV). Jesus was speaking of us. How much more should we forgive those who have scorned and abused us?

TO FORGIVE IS NOT TO CONDONE

Forgiveness does not mean you totally dismiss or condone wrong and hurtful behavior. Some people erroneously believe if they forgive someone, that person is released from paying any consequences. Just because you forgive someone does not mean you should allow that person to continue hurting you. It saddens me to think of how many women allow their spouses to repeatedly have extramarital affairs. These women have decided to just put up with it because somehow they think that makes them a good wife or a strong Christian. I'm talking about wives who condone years and years of infidelity with countless partners, not those who choose to forgive a truly repentant husband. Forgiving is not condoning bad behavior.

I actually listened to a radio interview with a woman who admitted that she and her husband have an open marriage. She spoke of how her family believed in working things out and exhausting every resource before calling it quits in a relationship. In an effort to keep her marriage, she decided she would allow her husband to date other people and even be intimate with them. She then said she believed in marriage.[3]

Folks, open marriage is an oxymoron. A marriage is a sacred union between a husband and wife. It cannot be shared with or intruded upon by anyone, even with spousal consent. If your spouse continues in infidelity, the marriage covenant is broken.

If there are no consequences to bad behavior, there will be no change. Forgiveness is not saying, "What you did to me doesn't matter." Yes, it *does* matter. If it didn't matter, forgiveness would be unnecessary. Forgiveness requires an honest appraisal of the harm done. It acknowledges the act as being wrong and forgives it anyway, but it never condones it.

You would not believe what supposedly strong Christian women would tell me when they counseled me by e-mail or on unexpected phone calls. I heard countless times, "All men cheat." Or, "Men with power and influence will always cheat." Or, "That's just the way it is. Just enjoy your status and your money." Or, "Know that you may not be the only lady, but you are the first lady." There were so many, but this one took the cake. A mother in the church told me, "A man will be a man." *Seriously?*

I honestly believe this thinking perpetuates infidelity in the church. It's almost giving men a pass to sin. There were people who expected me to condone infidelity in my marriage as an act of forgiveness. God did not require me to condone sin, nor does He require that of you. I eventually forgave those who hurt me, but I could not abide a marriage with continued infidelity.

The same scenario holds true for battered women and men. A battered person often believes that if she truly loves the person, she should stay in the abusive situation. Or she may think forgiving the abusive spouse means remaining in the marriage. There have been funerals for people who stayed in physically abusive marriages. Emotional abuse can be just as dangerous. Forgiving can mean loving from a distance.

REMEMBER GOD FORGAVE US

In Matthew 18 Jesus told a parable about a king who sought to settle the debts his servants owed him. One servant owed a particularly large sum of money, and when the king summoned the man, the servant was told his wife, children, and belongings were to be sold to satisfy his debt. The servant fell to his knees and begged the king for mercy, promising to pay back all he owed. The king took pity on the man and forgave his debt in full.

But when the servant left the king, he came across a man who owed him money. It was a small sum in comparison to what he owed the king. But the servant grabbed the man and began to choke him while demanding to be paid what he was owed. Just as the servant had done, the debtor fell on his knees and promised to pay up. But the servant refused and had the man thrown in prison until he could pay in full. The other servants who watched this transpire were upset and informed the king of what happened.

Matthew 18:32–35 says, "Then the master called the servant in. 'You wicked servant,' he said, 'I canceled all that debt of yours because you begged me to. Shouldn't you have had mercy on your fellow servant just as I had on you?' In anger his master turned him over to the jailers to be tortured, until he should pay back all he owed. This is how my heavenly Father will treat each of you unless you forgive your brother from your heart."

The world is full of I-forgot-where-I-came-from people. I believe strongly that your sin exposes your area of need. And when—not if—your weaknesses are exposed, that revelation is an act of love from God. He reveals your imperfections so you can get right and be ready when Christ comes.

We need to constantly remember how God delivered and protected us. Time and time again I've seen women who become pregnant out of wedlock face ridicule from their friends and family members. Some are even ostracized. But the crazy thing is, many of those friends and family members made the same mistake; they just did not get pregnant. God requires us to sincerely forgive to the same measure we have been forgiven.

I knew of a woman who was devastated by her husband's infidelity. She wanted to divorce him and was having a very hard time with the prospect of forgiving him. She eventually fell into a deep depression. Later it was discovered that *she* had been cheating on her husband at the same time he was cheating on her. She was never caught, yet she could not forgive her husband.

The Word of God says, "To whom much is given, from him much will be required" (Luke 12:48, NKJV). If we really took the time to look at the man or woman in the mirror, we would see our imperfections and remember we are not as good or perfect as we portray ourselves to be. We must have an attitude of gratitude toward God for not giving us what we deserve but instead allowing us to walk in supernatural grace. Let's afford that same grace and mercy to others.

There is a story of a mom who ran into the bedroom when she heard her seven-year-old son scream. She found his two-year-old sister pulling his hair. She gently released the little girl's grip and said comfortingly to her son, "There, there. She didn't mean it. She doesn't know that hurts." He nodded his acknowledgment, but as she turned to leave the room, the little girl screamed. When the mom turned, she saw that her son was now pulling his little sister's hair. When the little boy caught his mom's glance, he said, "She does now!"

I've gained so much compassion for others who have gone through or are going through divorce. Before my own experience I could not comprehend a Christian couple breaking up. I would often say, "Divorce is not an option!" I used to be extremely harsh and dogmatic toward those who sought a divorce. "God hates divorce" was my mantra. I had no concept of the spiritual and emotional abuse that often takes place behind closed doors, even within Christian marriages. It wasn't until I got my hair pulled that I truly understood.

Please don't get me wrong. I still believe in the sanctity of marriage. And I don't believe every couple faced with infidelity will, or should, end up divorced. But every situation is unique. I realize now that one size doesn't fit all when it comes to dealing with infidelity. Both parties must be willing to work at reconciliation by any means necessary.

A dear friend of mine greatly valued marriage and family. Unfortunately her husband unexpectedly handed her divorce papers. She was totally blindsided. He left her and moved across the country. Her family told her divorce is not an option, just as I used to do. But my friend was totally bewildered because he left her. Short of her begging him to stay, what was she to do? He staunchly refused to return.

The constant judgment from friends and family caused her unnecessary stress. She needed love and support during the most devastating time of her life. Her husband abandoned her, yet she was being judged.

Jesus understood the emotional and spiritual pain of infidelity. He said in Matthew 19 that God allowed divorce due to adultery because of the hardness of people's hearts (vv. 7–10). There are many occasions when the adulterous party will want to continue being unfaithful and develops a hard heart toward his or her spouse. Because of the hardness of that person's heart, God allows divorce.

God does not condone child abuse, which is why He does not require one of His children to remain in a marriage plagued by infidelity. We are living in a day and age when infidelity can be deadly because of the prevalence of sexually transmitted diseases. Jesus understood this; therefore we have Matthew 19. We must not judge someone else's action if we have never walked in his shoes. We must judge only according the standard of the Word, not according to our personal opinion. The Word is clear that God allows divorce, though it is not what He originally intended.

FORGIVE AND FORGET? YEAH, RIGHT.

I've heard countless times that we must forgive and forget. It's true that we must forgive, but it is almost impossible to forget a bad episode in our life. Instead of dwelling on the hurt we experienced, we must figure out what God is trying to teach us. If we forget, we may be setting ourselves up for an encore of the same painful experience.

I firmly believe that forgiving does not mean forgetting. Our memory bank serves an important purpose. It alerts us when situations arise that could possibly yield similar outcomes. However, I do believe that if we sincerely forgive, the pain of the offense will not persist. Eventually we will be able to live our lives without thinking about the hurt every day.

There were times when my mind would not allow me to forget. I honestly thought I would never rid myself of the pain of my husband's rejection and betrayal. Each day was filled with depressing thoughts and vivid memories of the atrocities he committed. Although I never forgot what happened, the memory lost its sting after a while.

Proverbs 4:23–27 tells us, "Keep thy heart with all diligence; for out of it are the issues of life. Put away from thee a froward mouth, and perverse lips put far from thee. Let thine eyes look right on, and let thine eyelids look straight before thee. Ponder the path of thy feet, and let all thy ways be established. Turn not to the right hand nor to the left: remove thy foot from evil" (KJV). It is extremely important not to get caught up in the pain. Modern technology allows disgruntled employees and scorned wives to post their stories online and let the world judge who is right and who is wrong. We must be extremely careful not to get caught up in the way the world operates. If we keep perpetuating the hurt, we will never get to the place of healing.

That means I cannot participate in gossip because I must guard my heart. I cannot befriend any and everyone, because evil communications corrupt good manners. If we purpose in our hearts to never forget the pain, we are damaging our lives. But if we allow healing to take place, although we don't forget the wrong done, we walk in the freedom of peace and joy.

I know a man who went through a bitter divorce. He has held on to the pain for many years. Because he constantly rehearses the ways his ex-wife hurt him, he has resigned himself to never marry again. He doesn't think he can trust anyone again. He has allowed his ex-wife's actions to imprison his happiness and destiny. "Where the Spirit of the Lord is, there is freedom" (2 Cor. 3:17). There will be freedom when you forgive.

Forgiving is psychologically healthy

The Bible says, "Follow peace with all men, and holiness, without which no man shall see the Lord: looking diligently lest any man fail of the grace of God; lest any root of bitterness springing up trouble you, and thereby many be defiled" (Heb. 12:14–15, KJV). This passage reflects a truth that many people don't fully realize. Unforgiveness affects people psychologically. Bitterness and resentment can cause obsessive anger and even debilitating depression. I've known people who entertained resentment for so many years they developed an imbalanced view of life.

I like the way author Lee Strobel puts it: "They don't hold a grudge as much as the grudge holds them."[4] When we decide not to forgive, we allow the person who wronged us to continue to hurt us. The root of bitterness becomes a ball and chain we drag with us throughout our lives. If we view life from an unbalanced perspective, we won't be able to recognize new opportunities available to us. God never intended for us to get stuck in our past. He wants us to sing a new song while He does a new thing. The hurt of yesterday should not be the hurt of today. Yesterday's hurt should be a vehicle for strength and compassion.

"As [a man] thinks within himself, so he is" (Prov. 23:7, NAS). If you constantly think about pain and hurt, you become pain and hurt. I have heard it said many times: hurting people hurt people. This is absolutely true. A dear friend of mine had a really devastating childhood. He has never released the pain of the past. When I see him, his countenance is downcast. He seldom smiles or laughs, and his posture is stooped. It literally seems as if a dark cloud is hovering over him. Although his childhood was decades ago, the scars are still evident today.

The psychological effects of unforgiveness not only harm the person, but they also harm the people connected to the unforgiving person. Children and spouses of unforgiving people can also take on a hopeless or angry disposition. Heaviness breeds heaviness.

Forgiving is physically healthy

"For wrath killeth the foolish man" (Job 5:2, KJV). Unforgiveness can kill. Spiritual warfare manuals are now linking many diseases to unforgiveness. Did you know unforgiveness has been linked to cardiovascular disease, high blood pressure, and even cancer? The *New York Times* reported that a wealth of data suggests chronic anger is so damaging to the body that it ranks with or even exceeds cigarette smoking, obesity, and a high-fat diet as a powerful risk factor for premature death.[5] The Word of God provides the antidote: "A cheerful heart is good medicine, but a crushed spirit dries up the bones" (Prov. 17:22).

My sister once worked with a woman who was notorious for being mean. Most people wanted to stay as far away from her as possible. Her disposition was very unpleasant, and she was vindictive. While everyone was moving away from this particular woman, my sister felt the leading of the Holy Spirit to minister to her. Over time she allowed my sister to peer beyond her brash, toughened exterior.

My sister realized her coworker harbored a great deal of unforgiveness from severe emotional pain and abuse she had experienced. Just when their friendship was beginning to grow, this woman discovered she had cancer. Praise God, the woman came to know Christ before she passed into eternity. But I can't help but wonder whether she became ill because she spent so many years nurturing an unforgiving spirit.

Studies have shown that forgiving others reduces stress-producing anger and improves mental, emotional, and physical health. That's right: forgiveness significantly reduces stress. Holding a grudge can place the same strains on your body—tense muscles, elevated blood pressure, increased sweating—as a major stressful event. So even for health reasons, holding a grudge is not worth it at all. Forgiveness also increases one's sense of control. Forgiving someone who wronged you can make you feel in control of the offending situation and your life. You develop emotional confidence to get through any difficulty, and you're less likely to panic when other hurtful situations arise.[6]

Finally, forgiveness is good for your heart—literally. One study from the *Journal of Behavioral Medicine* found forgiveness to be associated with lower heart rate and blood pressure as well as stress relief. This can bring long-term health benefits. A later study found forgiveness to be positively associated with five measures of health: physical symptoms, medications used, sleep quality, fatigue, and somatic complaints. It seems forgiveness also reduced depressive symptoms, strengthened spirituality, improved conflict-management skills, and relieved stress, which all have a significant impact on overall health.[7] Who knew?

Forgiving is spiritually healthy

For Christians unforgiveness can delay or deny answers to our prayers. A grudge is a weed that chokes off the sustenance our prayers need. Refusing to forgive is a sin in itself, and sin distances us from God. Forgiveness is a global concept. When we forgive others, God can forgive us. Even in the Lord's Prayer, our model prayer, Jesus included a forgiveness clause: "And forgive us our debts, as we forgive our debtors" (Matt. 6:12, KJV).

Jesus went on to admonish, "For if you forgive men when they sin against you, your heavenly Father will also forgive you. But if you do not forgive men their sins, your Father will not forgive your sins" (Matt.

6:14–15). It is clearly taught in the solemn words of our Savior that Christians who will not forgive will not be forgiven by their heavenly Father. Don't let unforgiveness hinder your communion with or service to God. All of your praying is useless unless you forgive others who may have wronged you.

Romans 4:8 says, "Blessed is the man to whom the Lord will not impute sin" (KJV). What a wonderful scripture. I am sure when we think of this verse, we envision sexual sin, violence, theft, and the like. But unforgiveness is a sin as well. Holding grudges or enmity against others may seem "small" when compared with drunkenness, stealing, or lying. But in God's sight, sin is simply sin.

SEE THROUGH THE EYES OF CHRIST

I love what Christian author Lewis Smedes said about the power of forgiveness. He wrote, "When you forgive someone, you slice away the wrong from the person who did it. You disengage that person from his hurtful act. You recreate him."[8] Let's really think about this. After Peter denied Jesus three times and behaved as a sinner instead of a disciple, some would think Jesus wouldn't have had anything to do with him. But Jesus forgave Peter (John 21:15–17). And as a result, Peter was changed—in fact, transformed! The man who denied Jesus preached boldly on the Day of Pentecost, and thousands came to know Christ as their Savior as a result (Acts 2).

Our forgiveness may make it possible for someone to repent and change. I like the way Randall O'Brien put it, "The question is not, 'Should I forgive if he doesn't repent?' It's 'Can he repent if I don't forgive?'"[9] Unforgiveness could be the very thing keeping a spouse from repenting. Forgiveness may be the tool that brings healing and unity in the marriage.

I believe in the power of forgiveness wholeheartedly. But as I said before, it is a process. One of the steps that can lead us to true forgiveness is found in the Sermon on the Mount. Jesus said, "You have heard it said that you are to hate your enemies, but I say to you, love your enemies. Pray for those who despitefully use you." (See Matthew 5:43–44.) So the first step in the process of forgiveness is to pray for the person who hurt you. *Wow.*

At times praying for someone who wronged you can be as distressing and distasteful as the event that created the need for forgiveness. But you have to press in prayer. You will find that the more you pray for the person who betrayed you, the more your heart will soften. It will become nearly impossible for you to hate the person who wronged you when you are praying for him, because your heart has not only overcome the hurt, but it has also been strengthened by it.

We must see our enemies as God sees them. We need to think about why they may have committed such hurtful acts. As a pastor I am constantly reminding church members and leaders alike that people's negative behavior and actions are usually linked to some deep-seated hurt or dysfunction. We must learn to respond differently to those who do hurtful things. This is why in Luke 6 Jesus commanded us to do good to those who hate us and to bless those who curse us (vv. 27–28). Jesus also said in Matthew 18:15–17 that when we are hurt, we are to go to the person who hurt us. We, the innocent party, are to initiate reconciliation. Forgiveness involves action!

You see, part of forgiveness is recognizing our contribution to the problem. Of course those who suffered a brutal attack, lost a loved one to random violence, were abused, or, perhaps, defrauded aren't to blame for the wrongs committed against them. I am talking about those who have experienced relational discord at church, work, or home. More often than not we share part of the blame for the breakdown. Perhaps we were mean, jealous, harsh, or self-centered. We need to recollect our contribution to the problem as we embrace Jesus's command to forgive. Few things accelerate the peace process more than humbly admitting our own wrongdoing and asking for forgiveness.

FORGIVE BECAUSE JESUS FORGAVE

Colossians 3:13 paints a clear picture of the role forgiveness must play in our lives. It says, "Bear with each other and forgive whatever grievances you may have against one another. Forgive as the Lord forgave you." As Christians we know God forgave us, but the magnitude of that fact is sometimes lost on us. In her book *Living Beyond Yourself*, author and speaker Beth Moore recalls a moment when God allowed her to recognize the incredible power of forgiveness.

> I will never forget watching an evening talk show featuring the story of the parents and killer of a young college student. The killer was his best friend. The weapon was high alcohol content inside a speeding automobile. What made this particular feature prime-time viewing? The parents had forgiven the young driver. And if that was not enough, they had taken him in as their own. This young man sat at the table in the chair which was once occupied by their only son. He slept in the son's bed. He worked with the victim's father, teaching seminars on safety. He shared their fortune and supported their causes. He spoke about the one he had slain in ways only someone who knew him intimately could have. Why did these parents do such a thing? Because it gave them peace.
>
> The interviewer was amazed; I was amazed. I kept trying to put myself in the parents' position—but I could not. Then, as the tears streamed down my cheeks, I heard the Spirit of God whisper to my heart and say: "No wonder you cannot relate. You have put yourself in the wrong position. You, my child, are the driver." God was the Parent who not only forgave, but also invited me to sit at His table in the space my Savior left for me. As a result, I have peace.[10]

That story literally sends chills through me. You can't operate in that level of forgiveness unless you have Christ in your life. Forgiveness is definitely a process. We all have heard lip service at one time or another. A person can easily say he forgives someone, but if he has not gone through the process in his heart, he is speaking empty words. It is very possible for you to think you have forgiven when you have not. When you have truly forgiven someone, you no longer seek to get even or punish the person. You give up the desire to see them "get what's coming to them," and you can sincerely pray that God forgives and blesses them.[11]

When you are able to genuinely look at the person who wronged you without rehearsing what he did, then you are doing great. When you can pray for the person and bless him with a genuine and sincere heart, you are definitely walking in forgiveness.

My process of forgiving took more than two years. Boy was it painful— even grueling at times. I chose to forgive, and now I am free from the grip Satan had on my mind and blessings. I am no longer held captive in Satan's prison of hurt and bitterness. Instead I am living in the freedom and liberty of the Holy Spirit, who brings favor, stability, and peace.

CHAPTER
7

ATTITUDE
DETERMINES ALTITUDE

I heard a minister preach a sermon about the vulture and the hummingbird, and the message has stuck with me. It offers such a clear picture of a truth I have discovered—that we all find what we are looking for.

Both the hummingbird and the vulture fly over our nation's deserts. Vultures instinctively seek rotting flesh. They thrive on that diet. But hummingbirds ignore the smelly carrion, instead looking for the colorful blossoms of desert flora. The vultures live on remnants of a past life; they consume what is dead and gone. But hummingbirds feed on what is alive. They fill themselves with freshness and vitality. Each bird finds what it is looking for. Ultimately we all do.[1] Our attitude has everything to do with what we receive in life.

Although there are several definitions of the word *attitude*, I want to highlight only two in this chapter. The first definition is a "manner, disposition, feeling, position with regard to a person or thing; a tendency or orientation, especially of the mind."[2] The second definition is a "position or posture of the body appropriate to or expressive of an action, emotion."[3] In short, an attitude is in inward belief that causes an outward expression.

I read a story once about a man who was taking flying lessons. Riding in the copilot's seat, the man noticed that the pilot kept looking at one of the instruments, so he asked what it was. The pilot said the instrument was called an altimeter, and it determined his altitude. He said in flying, the altitude of the plane is the position of the aircraft in relation to the horizon. When the airplane is climbing, it has a "nose high" altitude because the nose of the plane is pointed above the horizon. When the aircraft is diving, it has a "nose down" altitude. Because the performance of the airplane depends on its altitude, it is necessary to change the altitude in order to change the performance.[4]

Wow! The performance of an airplane depends on its altitude. I believe the same principle applies to our altitude in life. Our attitude determines our altitude. Our circumstances should not dictate our success or failure. Environment does play a significant part in the development of a person's perception of life. However, we each can choose whether to succeed or fail *despite* our environment or circumstance.

How do you respond to unfair or hopeless situations? Do you give up and believe the lie that life will never improve? The key to our success is our attitude in the face of trials. Let's look at a great example of a man of God who was able to maintain the right attitude in the midst of great loss and great pain: David.

In 1 Samuel 29 David had gotten tired of running from Saul, who was trying to kill him, so he and his men had settled in the land of the Philistines, in a region called Ziklag. David had earned the trust of Achish, son of the Philistine king of Gath. But when the Philistines decided to go to war against Israel, the commanders of the army disapproved of David and his mighty army fighting alongside them, fearing that David would turn against them and fight for Israel.

David and his men were sent back to Ziklag, but when they arrived they found their camp marauded and burned. The Amalekites had taken their wives and children captive and looted their possessions. David and his men wept bitterly until they had no more strength to weep. Traumatized and discouraged, the men began to blame David for their loss. Some were even conspiring to stone David. Yet in the midst of such heartbreak and discord, the Bible says David "found strength in the LORD his God" (1 Sam. 30:6)

David and his army had earned a reputation as fierce warriors. These men were undefeatable, fearless, skilled soldiers. When David wanted the hand of Saul's daughter in marriage, Saul demanded one hundred Philistine foreskins as payment, assuming David would be killed in the process (1 Sam. 18:25). To Saul's surprise, David not only returned alive but also brought with him two hundred Philistine foreskins. David and his men knew how to take charge and get the job done. All that skill, strength, and courage, however, could not help them cope with the loss of their families and possessions. They had to face the humbling truth that they were helpless and needed God.

When we were undergraduates at the University of Maryland–Baltimore County (UMBC), my twin sister, Rená, and I contracted the mumps. My sister enjoyed her short sabbatical from school. She kicked her feet up, watched television, and got plenty of rest. I on the other hand contracted meningitis from a complication of the mumps. My brain swelled significantly, which brought on terrible headaches. I also suffered severe back pain and lost quite a bit of weight. I spent several days in the hospital then was stuck at home on bed rest.

My father is a Recon Marine who fought in the Vietnam War and received the prestigious Purple Heart medal. He is an avid hunter and survivalist. He has always been a bold champion of justice and a lover of boxing and football. In short, he is a man's man. When I was growing up, it seemed he could fix anything and do whatever needed to be done. He stood head and shoulders above most of my friends' fathers. Yet my father never went to church when I was younger, always insisting that my mom, my sister, and I go without him each Sunday. He used to joke that God had a place reserved for him in heaven because Marines guarded the pearly gates.

I was at home still recovering from meningitis when my father walked slowly into my room. My daddy was the strongest man I had ever known, but when he came into my room, his face was somber and his eyes were sad. My father knelt beside my bed, reached for my hand, and held it gently. He did not say a word to me. My father bowed his head and then prayed for me as tears stained his cheeks. That was the first time I had ever seen my daddy pray for me. In that place of helplessness my father looked to God for strength. He made a choice to encourage himself in the Lord and keep an attitude of hopefulness and not despair.

Have you faced circumstances that left you weeping and discouraged? Have you felt like you were going to lose your mind from the stress of tragedy and heartbreak? Most of us can answer yes to at least one of these questions. Fortunately our circumstances don't dictate the future. Our attitude is the key to attaining the altitude we want in life, spiritually and in the natural.

As we saw in 1 Samuel 30, David's positive attitude was not contingent upon anyone's support or his great fighting ability. He remained consistent in his dependence on God. How did David manage to keep a positive attitude in the midst of such trying circumstances? Let's look closely at several principles that allowed David to keep the right attitude during his trial.

REMEMBER HOW GREAT GOD IS

David's family was coldheartedly kidnapped and his possessions viciously stolen from him. Yet David did not buckle under the pressure or surrender to the excruciating pain he felt. Many of us would have collapsed and given up on life in a situation like this. Some would have become bitter and angry with God and the world. David, instead, encouraged himself in the Lord. The word *encourage* in 1 Samuel 30:6 means "to strengthen, to make strong, to restore to strength."[5] David found strength in the Lord because he understood that God, not circumstances, defines life.

When I was younger, I interpreted the scripture "David strengthened himself in the LORD" to mean David told himself how special, smart, and anointed he was. No one else was there to lift David's spirit, so David lifted his own. I somehow thought the verse was saying we should speak those things that are not as though they were (Rom. 4:17). Just "name it and claim it," and everything would be all right.

While these may be popular clichés, they do not embody 1 Samuel 30:6. Encouraging yourself in the Lord means falling to your knees and telling God how wonderful, magnificent, amazing, and awesome *He* is, not how wonderful you are. In no way should you exalt yourself. It is a time to humble yourself before God and repent for not being all you should be while declaring who He is to you!

Worship is powerful. It changes the atmosphere from one of fear and heaviness to one of power and glory. Praise and worship are like a magnet that draws God nearer. There is a popular song by William Murphy that simply says, "Praise is what I do when I want to be close to You. I lift my hands in praise. Praise is who I am. I will praise Him while I can. I'll bless Him at all times."[6] I love those lyrics. When we worship God, our problems are dislodged from our thoughts and replaced by intimate reflection on God's grace and providence.

David said it this way in Psalm 34:1, "I will bless the LORD at all times: his praise shall continually be in my mouth"(KJV). When praise is continually in our mouths, there is no room for negative talk. The more His praises are in our mouths, the more we prophesy who God is to us. And the more we prophesy, the more He becomes who He says He is in our lives. Instead of saying, "I am sick" or "I am poor," say, "He is my healer" and "He is my provider."

Our words frame our world. You will have whatsoever you say (Mark 11:24). If you continually say you're losing your mind, eventually you will. But if you continually proclaim you have the mind of Christ, eventually you will. Recently a dear friend sent this message to her friends and family:

> Four years ago today Darryl did not wake up. Paramedics reported he had "no breath sounds, no heartbeat, no pulse…he's gone." Thank God for HIS report and not man's report! Darryl "slept" for three weeks and woke up on Resurrection weekend. Giving thanks

today for the "Miracle Man" and for waking up with "breath, heart-beat and pulse"! Make it a spectacularly blessed day!

—NICKY

Nicky, a prominent attorney and professor, awoke one night to her husband, Darryl, making gurgling sounds. She thought Darryl was snoring, but when she turned on the light and looked at him, he was foaming at the mouth, and his eyes had rolled back in his head. She couldn't believe what was happening. Darryl had been in optimum health since his All-Star football days in college. He was a successful financial planner who lived life to the fullest.

Nicky called 911 and administered CPR until the paramedics arrived. When the EMTs entered the room, they took one look at Darryl and said, "He's gone." Nicky couldn't fathom the idea that her college sweetheart and husband, the father of her children was gone. Thankfully the paramedics were able to revive him, and they rushed Darryl to the hospital.

Nicky called me, and I arrived at the emergency room before she did. When Darryl was stable, we went in to see him. The doctors had given grim reports, but we spoke only positive words over Darryl. As he lay in the ER, we spoke in Darryl's ear. We told him not to listen to the doctor's report but only to God's voice. We spoke life to Darryl and his spirit. Nicky continually kept praise and worship in her mouth throughout the grueling months that followed. And she did not allow anyone near Darryl who did not speak positively as he fought to regain his health.

Miraculously the man who "died" walks today. He is able to speak, albeit slowly. And though we are still praying for the complete restoration of his eyesight, Darryl is *alive*. Months after his ordeal Darryl told me he could hear everything we said in the emergency room when the paramedics said his organs had shut down and he would be nothing but a vegetable.

Darryl said he was supernaturally above us, looking down at his body, and he could hear us talking to him. What if Nicky had not encouraged herself and her husband in the face of Darryl's clinical death? What if Nicky hadn't kept worship on her lips throughout the battle? Nicky and

Darryl were able to endure the trial of their lives through their hope in God. You can do the same. Your attitude could be the very catalyst that brings life to your situation.

David's relationship with God grew exponentially through his worship. God draws close to those who draw close to Him (James 4:8). There is no way to have a bad attitude in the true presence of the Lord. In the midst of jubilant times, worship the Lord. In the depths of despair, worship the Lord. When you are intimate with God, He will strengthen you for the journey. He will orchestrate your blessing and breakthrough. And He will encourage you to move forward.

REMEMBER TO FOCUS ON GOD, NOT YOUR ENEMIES

Saul became jealous of David's anointing and sought to kill him. David, being the mighty warrior that he was, could have killed Saul numerous times, but David chose to allow God to vindicate him. However, David grew weary of constantly hiding from Saul. David didn't anoint himself, so why should Saul be jealous?

Though Saul was still in office, God had basically made him a lame duck when He anointed David king (1 Sam. 16). We see that a lot in our churches today. A leader becomes great in his own eyes, and because God can no longer work through him, He finds someone He can use. Thus many ministers are lame ducks, still in office but no longer called to lead the church into the future.

David fled to Ziklag, in the land of the Philistines, to get away from Saul's tyranny. The enemies of God—the Philistines—accepted him. David should have felt safe as the Lord's chosen king; instead he was in running for his life. Have you ever felt like David, when people seek to slander and hurt you because they are jealous of what God is doing in your life? Fortunately they can't stop God's plans for you; just like in David's life, God always has the final say.

David continued to exude a positive attitude even as he fled from Saul. The more you ignore your enemy, the less power he has. Conversely the more you acknowledge your enemy, the more power he has over you.

Jesus is our wonderful example. He spent forty days and forty nights in the wilderness while the devil relentlessly tempted Him. Jesus ignored the lavish proposals Satan made and countered the devil's deceptive promises by speaking only the pure Word of God.

I was in major transition. I was still married and going through counseling when I was removed from the staff of the church I had cofounded. My children still had health insurance, but I was no longer covered. I didn't have an updated résumé and was not prepared to reenter the job market. I felt lost and started to panic.

I decided to start a network marketing business, as there were still days when I couldn't even get out of bed, and my ongoing legal issues necessitated a flexible schedule. With the little strength I had, I worked the business from home. A friend from Tennessee helped me start a team, which consisted of friends and former church members. This gave me some financial security while I worked to get on my feet.

Being removed from the church was extremely painful, but I chose not to focus on my hurt but on the friends and family who were supporting me and my business. God was teaching me another lesson during this season. He was showing me how to trust Him. I learned how to encourage myself in God when others would not. I learned how to ignore those who hurt me and, more important, to sincerely love them. I refused to give power to the enemy. I ignored his whispers and continued to hearken to God's voice.

I honestly believe if we are the body of Christ, we should celebrate one another's achievements. We must eliminate the jealous spirit of Saul.

REMEMBER GOD'S LOVE

We read earlier that the Philistines rejected David's assistance in their battle with the Israelites because they feared he would turn on them. The irony is that if the Philistines had accepted David and his army, he would have missed the chance to recover his family and possessions. You see, when David returned home, the fires were still smoldering, so the

Amalekites' trail was still fresh. Those who took his family captive could not have been more than a day ahead.

No one enjoys the sting of rejection. The spiritual scars can last for many years if we are not careful. However, there are times when God will close doors of perceived opportunity in an effort to protect us. We often don't recognize God's hand in the moment we feel rejected. But if we remember that He loves us, we will be able to maintain a positive attitude and see our situation in light of His great plan for our lives, which is to prosper us and not to harm us (Jer. 29:11).

I have learned that the world is constantly looking for diamonds—people whose brilliance outshines the rest. The church today has adopted the same mentality. It honors and elevates the gifted and talented. I've noticed just the opposite in God's Word. God always chose the diamonds in the rough. He chose the least and the humble. If you have been rejected, please know God has not abandoned you. God may use that experience as part of His plan to elevate and promote you, depending on your attitude toward Him. Remembering God's love in the midst of rejection will help you keep the right attitude. It will help you see yourself cradled in His loving arms, where you are safe and protected.

When he had time to reflect, David must have been grateful that God allowed the Philistines to reject him. Hindsight works that way. We don't usually see how God is sparing us in the moment, only later. I've seen people get angry with God because a relationship didn't work out. It may take them a few years, but usually they realize if they had married that person, they would have been miserable. God always knows best. He will allow us to be rejected for a job or home loan, in a relationship or financial venture because God can see the ending in the beginning. What we want is not always what we need.

When my husband subjected me to the ultimate rejection, I found myself alone and wondering how I would get through. I felt horribly rejected and used, as though I was being thrown away because I was no longer needed. I wanted to give up and crawl under a rock, never to be seen or heard from again. But I could not help but remember God's love. I remembered how He kept me and my babies in good health when

Zach and I first moved to Florida and we couldn't afford health insurance. I remembered how He provided jobs for me so I could help pay the bills for our family. I remembered how God grew the ministry from four to more than eight thousand members. I knew that if God provided then, He could do it again. His mercies are fresh every morning, and His loving-kindness is better than life. Through my husband's rejection, I gained a deeper sense of acceptance from my God.

REMEMBER GOD'S PROMISES

When David was faced with what may have seemed like an impossible situation, he drew strength from his past experiences with God. When he encouraged himself in the Lord, David reflected on the numerous times God had demonstrated His love, guidance, and protection. David hearkened back to his days in the desert, when he learned to hear the voice of God while caring for the sheep. David remembered that God had anointed him to be king even though he wasn't walking in that calling yet. He recalled all the promises God whispered to him as he worshiped the Lord in the beauty of His holiness. You too must remember what God has done in your life and the promises He has given you. You must prophetically speak those promises over your life in order to renew your strength.

It was difficult for me to stop attending the church Zach and I founded. I remember the first time I didn't go to the church's New Year's celebration. They were always extravagant events that we spent months planning. A prominent bishop my husband and I knew asked me to attend, but I could not go. I felt it would be disingenuous for me to create the illusion that our family was healing. It had been only three months, and Zach was already preaching again though his family was still struggling. Why couldn't he stay at home with me and the kids and bring healing to our family?

I spent New Year's Eve at the home of a former church member and others who had left. There we began to discuss starting an outreach ministry. I can remember throwing out the name "Celebration of Life Ministries." We then began having monthly board meetings. The outreach ministry was quickly turning into a church on paper. Everyone was so excited. We had the momentum. Now we needed a place to worship.

As time passed, I started to feel less and less enthused about ministry. Within six months I told everyone I could not move forward with Celebration of Life because I was still too weak in my spirit. I could definitely feel the disappointment of some members of the group, but I knew I would eventually crash if I stepped out too soon.

I was in an unfamiliar place. I began questioning my life and my walk with God. I started to wonder whether my calling was wrapped in my husband's purpose. I thought maybe I should finish graduate school, get a secular job, and call it a day.

I was certain I would never pastor again. I had no desire to deal with church folk. I loved the Lord but didn't want anything to do with the institution of church. I told God and everyone else I would never pastor again. At least that's what I thought.

I began reading a journal I kept of prophetic words that had been spoken over my life through the years. God reminded me that before I was in my mother's womb, He knew me. None of what I had experienced took God by surprise. The Lord reminded me that my purpose was wrapped in Him not man. I had been saved most of my life and had a strong relationship with the Lord before my husband ever set foot in a church. I was an ordained deaconess, minister, elder, and pastor. God had called *me* to ministry, not only my husband.

God has a perfect will for our lives. Although we are all imperfect and sometimes connect with people who seem to take us off course, those missteps don't negate or derail our purpose. God allows detours in our lives, but He is the spiritual GPS, and He has the power to reroute the course so we reach our destination. I was born to minister, which means I was born to serve others. I was born with compassion for people and the desire to see them succeed. I was born to be a servant of the Lord.

Let every stumbling block become a stepping-stone to your destiny. I allowed the prophetic words I read in my journal to permeate my soul and spirit. Before long Majestic Life Institute emerged as an outreach ministry to engage in evangelism and disciple new believers. It's funny how God disregarded my determination to never pastor again. From Majestic Life Institute, He created Majestic Life Church.

REMEMBER PAST DELIVERANCE

David killed a lion and bear as a *child*. It was no surprise that he grew to be a great warrior. David had countless memories of God protecting him during perilous times throughout his life. Those experiences bolstered David's faith to believe God had the power to deliver him yet again.

I was twenty-three years old when I got married. In a little over two months, I was pregnant with my first child. I gave birth to my second child eleven months after my daughter was born. I was a newlywed with two babies and only twenty-five when our pastor sent my husband and me to Florida to start a church. Before we left Maryland for Orlando, my six-month-old son was diagnosed with cerebral palsy. We had no family, no jobs, and no money in Orlando. The stress was unbearable at times, and I thought a nervous breakdown was imminent.

We started the church in a hotel. For the first three years I worked secular jobs to pay the bills while Zach stayed home to work on the ministry. From the hotel we leased a storefront and had a third baby. We then purchased an old Baptist church building, which was followed by the purchase of more land and the construction of two buildings. We had a fourth baby, and I began cohosting our national television ministry. All of this happened within just five years. For those of you wondering, the pill and patch birth control methods did not work for me. God sent these babies, but they left me with almost no time to rest or recharge emotionally.

Zach was a shrewd businessman. He loved to negotiate, and he loved wealth. He was adamant that we never stay in one home more than two years. We moved ten times within eleven years. I was tired—mentally, emotionally, and physically. The abnormal became normal to me. During this fast-paced journey, I lost my identity. Smokey Robinson's song "Tracks of My Tears" describes the state I was in. On the outside I was laughing loud and hearty, but deep inside I was blue.

Because of my whirlwind journey in ministry, when it was time for me to start Majestic Life Church, I knew what to do. It is funny to think back on all the hats I wore during those early days at the church my husband and I cofounded. Because we could not afford to pay an attorney, I filed the paperwork myself for the church to apply for 501(c)(3) nonprofit status. I created the logo and developed the departments. I helped launch a program that aired locally on late-night television. I took calls on the prayer line too.

I learned a lot from my husband. He had big dreams and was always determined to make them a reality. So I was able to pull from the past to further my future with Majestic Life Church.

INQUIRE OF THE LORD

In 1 Samuel 30 David was faced with a desperate situation. His family had been taken captive, and some of his troops were so distraught about their loss they were conspiring to stone David. In the midst of this turmoil, David did one of the wisest things anyone can do: "David inquired of the Lord, saying, 'Shall I pursue this troop? Shall I overtake them?' And He answered him, 'Pursue, for you shall surely overtake them and without fail recover all'" (1 Sam. 30:8, NKJV).

David sought guidance from God before taking action against the Amalekites. When God gave His answer, David obeyed straightaway. David strengthened himself in the Lord. He strengthened his relationship with the Lord. He strengthened his worship and prayer. Then, when David got in proper standing with God, he inquired of the Lord. In contrast when Saul was in need of answers, the Bible says he sought the counsel of a witch (1 Sam. 28:3–25). David knew the right source for answers and strategy.

In order to develop and maintain a positive attitude, we must listen for God's voice. The enemy wants to distract us with his deceitful whispers. He wants to bring hate, depression, contention, and strife. When you spend time with the Lord, you will discern His voice, and a stranger's voice you will not follow (John 10:1–5).

It is important to notice that David sought the Lord immediately. We have a tendency to look to our friends, the mother of the church, a prophetic conference, or Christian television or radio for answers rather than going first to God. Man's answers are inferior to God's and will trip you up every time.

When you inquire of the Lord, He will answer. God answered David and told him to pursue the enemy, "for you shall surely overtake them and without fail and recover all" (1 Sam. 30:9, NKJV). God not only gave David instructions, but He also gave him a promise that he would be victorious. But hearing from God was only the first step. David had to obey. We can't say no when God says go.

When God told David to pursue his enemies, overtake them, and recover all, He never told David how much help he would have. God never told David that two hundred of his six hundred men were going to become faint and refuse to go with him (1 Sam. 30:10). God seldom tells us everything because He knows that too much information can lead to doubt and disobedience.

We know the story of Joseph, who had an amazing dream in which he saw his family bow to him. Joseph did not know he would experience many years of hardship before that dream became a reality. Had he known, I wonder whether he would have shared his dream with his brothers.

When God speaks to you, do what He says, whatever it is. You may lose money and friends along the way, but if God gave the instruction, He will give you the provision so His glory will be manifest. In Jeremiah 32:27 God said, "Behold, I am the LORD, the God of all flesh: is there any thing too hard for me?" (KJV). Nothing is too hard for the Lord.

When David received his instructions from the Lord, he and his men went in pursuit of the Amalekites. Along the way they found an Egyptian who had been enslaved by the Amalekites. The man led David right to the Amalekites' camp. David and his men had to fight from dusk until dawn—they were not just handed the victory—but the Bible says they recovered everything the Amalekites had taken. "Nothing was missing:

young or old, boy or girl, plunder or anything else they had taken. David brought everything back" (1 Sam. 30:19).

After years of walking with the Lord and seeing God deliver him time and again, David wrote: "He only is my rock and my salvation: he is my defence; I shall not be moved. In God is my salvation and my glory: the rock of my strength, and my refuge, is in God. Trust in him at all times; ye people, pour out your heart before him: God is a refuge for us" (Ps. 62:6–8, KJV).

David, like all of us, was far from perfect. Yet his relationship with God is still a shining illustration of what it means to walk by faith. He trusted God above all others, and God acknowledged his attitude of dependence by constantly providing for and elevating him. David's attitude determined his altitude. His life is a testament that all things are possible with God. We can be encouraged by David's example as we live our own life for God.

CHAPTER
8

STAND ON
GOD'S WORD

We live in a society that is filled with unprecedented pressures. This is the first generation that is not better off financially than its parents.[1] Christians are getting divorced at roughly the same rate as nonbelievers.[2] Our children have to deal with drugs, guns, and sex in schools, and they are barraged with music that promotes alternative lifestyles, promiscuity, greed, violence, and lust. Our husbands and sons are inundated with pornography in commercials and movies.

The cares of this life can be extremely distracting. Many people work eight hours a day, then come home to prepare meals, do laundry, clean the house, and care for the children. They face financial pressure, marital pressure, and even pressure to look good. Men and women alike go to the gym trying to look like nineteen-year-olds, and it never seems to work. So more and more people are turning to cosmetic surgery in hopes of meeting a standard of beauty that is virtually unattainable.

The stress we live under can drain the very life out of us and cause us to become weary. The word *weary* means to be exhausted in strength, endurance, vigor, freshness, patience, tolerance, or pleasure.[3] When you're exhausted of all these emotional resources, you can want to give up altogether.

God's Word forewarns us that we may face overwhelming pressures when we are doing the right things. Galatians 6:9 says, "And let us not be weary in well doing: for in due season we shall reap, if we faint not" (KJV). When we are on the right track, the enemy will form weapons to distract us from reaching our destination. The enemy does not want us to grab hold of who we are in Christ.

The Lord is not surprised by anything the enemy uses to get us away from God's plan for our lives. God allows these obstacles to come so our faith may be strengthened (James 1:2–4). The only way to avoid becoming weary in well doing is to stay in the Word of God and stand on His promises.

SATAN COMES TO STEAL THE WORD

The enemy never wants you in a place where the Bible can produce fruit in your life. In the Gospel of Mark Jesus told the following parable:

> The farmer sows the word. Some people are like seed along the path, where the word is sown. As soon as they hear it, Satan comes and takes away the word that was sown in them. Others, like seed sown on rocky places, hear the word and at once receive it with joy. But since they have no root, they last only a short time. When trouble or persecution comes because of the word, they quickly fall away. Still others, like seed sown among thorns, hear the word; but the worries of this life, the deceitfulness of wealth and the desires for other things come in and choke the word, making it unfruitful. Others, like seed sown on good soil, hear the word, accept it, and produce a crop—thirty, sixty or even a hundred times what was sown.
>
> —MARK 4:14–20

This is why the apostle Paul's admonition in Galatians 6:9 is so important. It says if we faint not, in due season we shall reap a harvest. That harvest could be souls brought into the kingdom, restoration of your marriage or family, a supernatural job opportunity, emotional healing, or a release into a new area of ministry. So the assignment the Lord gave me for this chapter is to identify some of the obstacles the devil sets up in an attempt to test our faith and snatch the Word of God from us. We can't conquer what we don't confront, and we can't confront what we don't identify. So let's examine some of the reasons people do not stand on the Word of God in difficult times.

A hard heart

"Some people are like seed along the path, where the word is sown. As soon as they hear it, Satan comes and takes away the word that was sown in them" (Mark 4:15). The King James Version puts it this way: "And these are they by the way side, where the word is sown; but when they have heard, Satan cometh immediately, and taketh away the word that was sown in their hearts." The Lord sows His Word into the hearts of His people. But the Bible says when the seed is sown on the wayside, Satan comes immediately to steal it.

Why is the Word so quickly and easily taken from those on the wayside? In order to answer that question, we must understand the dynamics of the wayside. The wayside is the side or edge of a road or path. It is an area that people and animals constantly trample on. As a result, the ground is compacted and extremely hard. Sister Wayside is the same. She has dealt with trials and hardship all her life. She has gotten used to dysfunction and now has a defeated mentality. She believes the enemy has more power than he actually does.

Because Sister Wayside has been rejected and trampled upon by those she thought would love and protect her, she has become hardened and bitter. As a self-preservation mechanism, she has decided not to trust anyone. So Sister Wayside is skeptical of everyone and everything. She lacks joy and compassion. Sister Wayside no longer lives but merely exists.

There are times when she hears a word from the Lord, and it touches her spirit. She knows life can be better, and she wants better. The tragedy is, her heart is so hard that the Word cannot penetrate past the surface.

Usually, before she gets into her car to go home from church, the enemy has already taken the Word from her. This explains why some people can attend church every Sunday and not change their ways or obtain the promises of God.

Shallow relationship with God

"Others, like seed sown on rocky places, hear the word and at once receive it with joy. But since they have no root, they last only a short time. When trouble or persecution comes because of the word, they quickly fall away" (Mark 4:16–17). The Bible says that when the Word is sown on stony ground, it is received with gladness but endures for only a short time.

Mr. Stony is a real hoot. He is well known throughout the community and the church. Mr. Stony loves people and is the life of every party. When the Word is sown in Mr. Stony's life, he gets excited and shouts and dances all around the church. Mr. Stony wants to witness to everyone and testify of God's goodness. He receives the Word with gladness. Unfortunately, if something does not go the way Mr. Stony would like, he gets extremely offended.

Mr. Stony gets upset if the pastor doesn't recognize him, if someone sits in his seat, or if someone else is given the lead position on the praise team. Almost anything can cause Mr. Stony to get frustrated, and the enemy comes right up and quickly takes the Word he was so happy to receive.

Stony ground is not conducive for planting because it is too shallow for seeds to grow roots. Mr. Stony's relationship with the Lord is the same way. Mr. Stony depends on his pastor, Christian television, and ministry conferences to cultivate his relationship with the Lord. As a result, he is not rooted in the things of God. He is easily offended and hops from church to church because there is no stability in his walk with God. You can discern the spiritual maturity of a person by how well he can handle adversity and persecution. Those who are mature in Christ are deeply rooted in God, and the enemy cannot steal the Word easily.

The cares of this world

"Still others, like seed sown among thorns, hear the word; but the worries of this life, the deceitfulness of wealth and the desires for other things come in and choke the word, making it unfruitful" (Mark 4:18–19). Thorny ground is very dangerous for the Word. The seed is able to take root, but the thorns and weeds choke the seed.

We see this very clearly with First Lady Thorny. She is a real trip. First Lady Thorny is a busybody and micromanager. She has to have her hand in everything in the church. First Lady Thorny does not rest because she is too busy worrying and planning her next project. She is constantly trying to keep up with the Joneses and is in fierce competition with all the other churches in her area.

She equates her spirituality with the size of her bank account and the number of possessions she has. First Lady Thorny must have the best cars, clothes, and homes. Because First Lady Thorny is concerned with the cares of the world and lusts after deceitful riches, the Word she receives gets choked out. Her time is basically wasted because the Word sown in her life is not able to produce fruit. She knows Jesus's words in Mark 8:36 but does not truly understand what He meant when He said, "What will it profit a man if he gains the whole world, and loses his own soul?" (NKJV).

First Lady Thorny can quote Scripture and even preach. But her sermons and even the scriptures she recites are often manipulated to serve her purpose of gaining more prestige and worldly possessions. Therefore the Word does not bring life to her. The things of this world are temporal and should never be our focus. We must diligently pursue the true riches, which are spiritual and everlasting.

The Word thrives in good ground

"Others, like seed sown on good soil, hear the word, accept it, and produce a crop—thirty, sixty or even a hundred times what was sown" (Mark 4:20). Good ground is not too compacted; it has no stones, thorns, or weeds. The soil is full of nutrients to cultivate the Word. It allows the

Word to grow and produce strong roots that cannot be easily plucked up by the enemy.

Bishop Good Ground has been through a lot in his life. Yet through all of his ups and downs, he never turned his back on the Lord. He remained faithful in his walk with God and stayed committed to the work of the ministry.

Bishop Good Ground stands on the Word daily seeking instruction and direction. As a result of his deep-rooted relationship with God, Bishop Good Ground reaps harvest after harvest. He sees salvation in his family, financial blessings, and loved ones healed. Bishop Good Ground has faced trials and tragedies, but God kept him safe within a hedge of protection during those trying times. Because he has spent years standing on the Word of God, Bishop Good Ground is not stopped by traumatic episodes. The Word gives him strength to keep pressing forward. No matter what he may face, Bishop Good Ground is able to stand on God's promises with vigor.

Did you recognize yourself in any of those examples? God wants us to be rooted in His Word because He knows storms will come. We will all have a turn to deal with major challenges in life. I've heard it said that we all are either headed into, in the middle of, or coming out of a storm. We can weather those storms only if God's Word is planted deep in our hearts.

If you are not in the midst of a storm now, why not help someone who is going through. Stand in agreement with your brother or sister in Christ, as you believe the Word for deliverance and breakthrough.

Parents who have multiple children want each child to do well, and they are not satisfied if only three out of four children are thriving. If your children came home excited because they won medals at a school event, you would be thrilled. But what if one of your children came home empty-handed? Although you were excited for the children who won awards, you can't help but feel for the one who didn't win anything. You may wish you could turn back the clock and take your child's place in the event so he would win the prize.

We know that's not how life works. As parents all we can do is encourage our children and refuse to let them become disillusioned or depressed. We can tell them they may not have won today, but there is always tomorrow. I certainly feel this way about my natural children, but I also feel this way about my spiritual family. It is great when some of the members receive a breakthrough, but I want to see all of us walking in what God has promised.

THE RACE SET BEFORE US

The Bible is filled with metaphors, parables, and analogies that increase our faith for the journey God has us on. Repeatedly the Bible compares the Christian life to a race. We all know that when the Bible mentions something more than once, we need to pay attention because it is important.

When I think of a race, I think of rapid movement toward a goal. When runners are thirsty, they don't stop to relax as they get hydrated. They simply grab a drink in mid-stride. That is how our faith should be—always moving forward. If a runner is in a relay race, he is standing ready to catch the baton and run his leg of the race. That's how God wants our faith to be—in ready mode.

The Bible speaks of ten virgins who were waiting for the bridegroom. Five had oil in their lamps, and five did not. Half of the virgins were not ready, but the bridegroom did not wait (Matt. 25:1–13). If your faith is in ready mode at all times, you will be in position to receive what God has promised. Let me give you a brief example.

A young man confirmed a breakfast date and time with his girlfriend. Unfortunately, when he arrived to pick her up, she still had on her robe and slippers, and there were curlers in her hair. The man had two choices. He could wait for another thirty minutes until she was ready, or he could leave without her and pick up another friend for breakfast.

Just as the young man was on time, God also is always on time. God often knocks on our door expecting us to be ready, but too often we open the door in our spiritual robes and slippers. I can hear the Lord saying,

"Didn't I tell you your promise was coming? Didn't I tell you this was your season? I gave you My Word. Why aren't you ready?"

If God said you would have a successful business, why haven't you incorporated it, developed the business plan, or set up a website? Faith without works is dead (James 2:26). This is how many in the body of Christ abort their promise. When God gives us a promise, we must stand on that word and be prepared for God to bring it to pass.

A cloud of witnesses

"Wherefore seeing we also are compassed about with so great a cloud of witnesses, let us lay aside every weight, and the sin which doth so easily beset us, and let us run with patience the race that is set before us" (Heb. 12:1, KJV). When reading that scripture, we usually focus on the "lay aside every weight" part, but I want to focus on the cloud of witnesses.

I was always taught that the cloud of witnesses was saints who went to heaven to be with the Lord. As I studied that verse, I found out that the word *cloud* in this scripture means "many."[4] Like a "bunch" of grapes or a "heap" of fries, a "cloud" is basically a large quantity of a particular thing. The writer of Hebrews was saying there are a lot of witnesses in the stadium of heaven.

No matter which country is hosting, Olympic stadiums are huge and always packed during the games. Thousands of people fill the arena to watch the various events. There are usually many coaches, commentators, and past competitors among the spectators. Those former Olympians understand what the participating athletes are experiencing. They can bear witness to the fact that it is possible to get through the event because they have done it. But they have also set a standard. It is their record the new crop of athletes wants to break. Their accomplishments are what motivated the new generation to run, jump, skate, or row as fast or high or well as they possibly could.

The cloud of witnesses set a standard and a benchmark. I want to be one of the many witnesses. I want to be a witness who stands before you and says your life is not over because someone rejected you. God is faithful to His promise even when everyone else is not. I pray that anyone who goes through a situation similar to mine will realize their purpose remains intact during trials. I pray that I am able to encourage someone to do better and recover faster than I did, that my witness will help someone continue to move forward in God's purpose for her life.

Build your stamina

The Greek word for *race* used in Hebrews 12:1 is *agōn*, which means a place of assembly, a contest, an effort, anxiety, or conflict.[5] *Agōn* is also the root word for *agonia*, which means contention or fight.[6] Sometimes our faith walk will cause us anguish, but having the Word hidden in our hearts will give us the strength to persevere.

When I played basketball, the coach made us do an exercise called "suicides" to build up our stamina. We had to run laps and do conditioning training to stimulate muscle growth and strength. A race is not easy; it's a competition in which everyone wants to be victorious. So you have to run to win, and that takes endurance.

God wants you to be ready for the blessing. If God promised you a huge financial breakthrough, He will keep His promise. But He has to make sure you are ready to receive it, so He will put you through spiritual boot camp. He will stretch and pull you. And you may experience cramps and suffer strains. Athletes often encounter these kinds of difficulties as they train, but they learn to push through the pain. Likewise must a Christian learn how to press through the pain. You just have to hold on. It's only a matter of time before you get your second wind.

The second wind for a runner is when he pushes past the painful period and is rewarded with renewed strength, vigor, and focus. Oftentimes athletes are able to run harder and faster at the end of the race because of this second wind. I believe God is speaking to the body of Christ today to dig into His Word, eat and drink its substance, and allow God to supernaturally give you the strength to win.

RUN TO WIN

We must be careful not to become complacent in our walk with the Lord. In 1 Corinthians the apostle Paul again likens the Christian life to a race.

> Do you not know that in a race all the runners run, but only one gets the prize? Run in such a way as to get the prize. Everyone who competes in the games goes into strict training. They do it to get a crown that will not last; but we do it to get a crown that will last forever. Therefore I do not run like a man running aimlessly; I do not fight like a man beating the air. No, I beat my body and make it my slave so that after I have preached to others, I myself will not be disqualified for the prize.
>
> —1 CORINTHIANS 9:24–27

If we're going to run, we must run to win. We can't go through the motions. We must make our lives count. Bible teachers and preachers alike are often in danger of losing their races because they think they can teach the Word but not live it. No matter who we are, our walk with God deserves 100 percent effort.

I used to run track, and I was pretty good at the 100-, 200-, and 400-meter races. I wasn't good enough to compete in the Olympics. But if I had made up my mind to practice twelve hours a day, strength train, and push myself to the limit, I believe I would have passed the Olympic trials. But I wasn't willing to do that. I wasn't willing to do what it took to compete on the Olympic level. Therefore I could not get upset with those who made the sacrifices to train and thus reaped the reward. Neither can you get frustrated or envious when someone else is blessed if you did not give God your all and make sacrifices to spend time with Him.

You will run your race differently when you have set a standard for yourself. The Bible says we are to run in such a way as to win. Remember a race is a competition. Stop beating the air and remain focused. Have you written the vision and made it plain? Have you set goals? Are you spending time in the Word? In other words, have you done your part?

In the Book of Acts Paul prayed that he would finish the race and complete the task the Lord gave him. And he considered finishing the race worth the hardships and threats of prison that awaited him in every city he visited. He said his life was worth nothing to him if only he could complete the task of testifying to the gospel of God's grace (Acts 20:23–24).

Paul realized that the race wasn't about him. It's not about us either. Yes, God wants to bless you, but that should never be your focus. Our personal ambitions and considerations must be shelved. We cannot get our feelings hurt and people cannot rub us the wrong way if we decide that our lives belong to the Lord. After all, we're not running this race to win a house, a car, or any other material thing. Our goal is to advance God's kingdom.

We must "fix our eyes on Jesus, the author and perfecter of our faith, who for the joy set before him endured the cross, scorning its shame, and sat down at the right hand of the throne of God" (Heb. 12:2). In long-distance running there is a pacesetter who sets the tone for the race. Sometimes the pacesetter will be used to help another runner break a record.

Jesus is our pacesetter. He is our example. When you are running and can see the finish line but are growing tired, do not give up! "Consider him who has endured such opposition from sinful men, so that you will not grow weary and lose heart" (Heb. 12:3). The Christian walk is not a sprint; it's a marathon. It will require dedication, endurance, and faith. Jesus has already set the pace, so let us press toward His mark and finish the race.

PUT A PRAISE ON!

How can you praise God when your heart has been broken? How can you praise God when sickness took your child from you? How can you praise God when you have been diagnosed with an incurable disease? How can you praise God when you've lost everything you worked so hard for? *How?*

When the psalmist felt dejected and forsaken, when his enemies were taunting him and tears were his food night and day, he made this determination: "I will yet praise him, my Savior and my God" (Ps. 42:5, 11). Praising God may seem like the hardest thing to do when your world is falling apart, but putting on praise is the key to your breakthrough. Let me explain.

The Lord gives us a garment of praise in place of the spirit of heaviness, a garment that is worthy of praise. We see throughout Scripture that a garment represents covering. When the prodigal son left home, squandered his inheritance, and lived a riotous life, his father gave him a robe when he returned (Luke 15:22). The robe represented the father's love, mercy, and covering. We read in Genesis 37:3 that Jacob gave Joseph a coat of many colors because he was the son of his old age. The garment of many colors symbolized the father's favor.

We see in Isaiah 61:3 that we are to receive a garment of praise for the spirit of heaviness. The garment of praise clothes the children of God. The Father has made a designer's original for each of His children. My praise is different from my neighbor's praise. My garment of praise is unique, and our heavenly Father loves to see me wear it.

Although the garment of praise is seen outwardly, it greatly affects us inwardly. When the Lord removes the weight of heaviness from our lives, we literally become different. Have you ever watched how people behave when they put on a new outfit? They usually have a little pep in their step; they walk with a new level of confidence. When the Lord gives us a garment of praise, our entire disposition changes.

After my husband and I divorced, I got such a kick out of seeing people react to me when they happened upon me in the grocery store or at the mall. I would usually hear things like, "Oh, my goodness; wow, is that you?" Or, "Pastor Riva, you look great!" The surprised looks on their faces were priceless. They assumed I would be wearing the spirit of heaviness, but the Lord had given me a beautiful, tailor-made garment of praise. It clothed me from head to toe, and I would not dare leave home without it.

A GARMENT WORTHY OF PRAISE

A very talented fashion designer attends my church. She loves to create outfits of all sorts. In order for her vision to come to life, she must choose the right fabric for the garment. Wool won't flow like satin; taffeta is not as delicate as silk. The same is true with the garment of praise. The fabric had to be made of something strong enough to eradicate the spirit of heaviness. That is why the garment of praise is made of grace and mercy.

The grace of God is amazing, and His mercy is without compare. I'm sure you can't help but smile and feel joy when you think of how far the Lord has brought you. The prophet Jeremiah said the word of the Lord was like a fire shut up in his bones. It wore him out trying to hold it in

(Jer. 20:9). Our praise should be the same way. It should burn in our hearts like a fire.

We know that certain attire is suitable for certain occasions. Sweat pants are no more appropriate for a corporate office than a business suit is for a jog in the park. The garment of praise isn't like that. It can be worn in any setting; it is appropriate for all occasions. You can be alone at home, at work, in a department store, or at church—it doesn't matter. The garment of praise will be the right thing to wear.

Don't worry about looking undignified while praising God in your car. There is never a bad time to remind yourself of the goodness of Jesus. I am reminded of a song by the late Bishop Walter Hawkins called "What Is This?" He sang that whatever "it" was setting his soul on fire, "it" just wouldn't let him hold his peace. That's the Holy Spirit in the garment of praise. It won't let you hold your peace. You'll have to open your mouth and give Him glory.

Pastor Douglas Chukwuemeka from Phoenix, Arizona, has been a spiritual father to me since I was twenty-five years old. I love to see him wear his garment of praise. When Pastor Doug talks about how Jesus has kept him and First Lady Roslyn, his face lights up, and sometimes he lets out a shout. If he is in church, watch out. His garment of praise will be in full effect. He may just start singing, "When I think about Jesus and what He's done for me, when I think about His goodness and how He set me free, I can dance, dance, dance all night!"[1]

You may feel the same way. Just thinking about the goodness of Jesus makes you want to dance, dance, dance all night! Some of you can relate to me when I say that if the enemy had his way, I would have lost my mind. I could have become bitter and full of hate. Some of you can say you should have been strung out on drugs. Some of you know you could have contracted a deadly STD because of the promiscuous lifestyle you led. Or maybe you were in the military stationed in Afghanistan and God placed a hedge of protection around you. Whatever your "it" is, you have a praise because of it.

HONOR GOD WITH YOUR PRAISE

The garment of praise distinguishes you as a child of God. It is a regimental uniform that shows which army you belong to. It is like a coat in the natural; it will protect you against the elements. It will keep you warm when everything and everyone else is frigid, and cool when life turns up the heat. The garment of praise is comfortable and oh so beautiful.

No matter how devastating or hopeless your trial may be, God is able to turn it into triumph. *Triumph* is the act, fact, or condition of being victorious, or victory itself. *Triumph* also means a significant success or noteworthy achievement and the exultation resulting from victory.[2] The definition of triumph itself is enough to make you want to do a dance and give God praise.

The Word of God speaks of triumphing in praise. Psalm 106:47 says, "Save us, O LORD our God, and gather us from among the heathen, to give thanks unto thy holy name, *and to triumph in thy praise*" (KJV, emphasis added). And we read in Psalm 47:1–2, "Oh, clap your hands, all you peoples! Shout to God with the voice of triumph! For the LORD Most High is awesome; He is a great King over all the earth" (NKJV).

These two verses in Psalms highlight the fact that praise is extremely strategic for your victory. The Hebrew word for "triumph" in Psalm 106:47 is *shabach*, which means to address in a loud tone.[3] Second, the word translated the "voice of triumph" in Psalm 47:2 is *rinnah*, which is a creaking or shrill sound, shout of joy, gladness, rejoicing, or proclamation.[4] This type of triumph praise is *loud*!

I know the Lord receives our praise whether it is loud or soft, on key or off. But loud worship really captures the incredible triumph of the Lion of Judah, who has won the victory over Satan (Rev. 5:5). And the worship that encircles the throne is *loud* (Rev. 5:11–12). There are plenty of opportunities to worship the Lord with quiet reverence, but there are times when we need to praise the Lord with all of our might. The Bible speaks of David praising God with all of his heart—to the point that he danced right out of his clothes (2 Sam. 6)!

I recently listened to an interview in which country singer Shania

Twain discussed her husband's infidelity. She said deep depression kept her in bed for days on end. I can totally relate. I spent days upon days unable to get out of bed. My chest was tight, and I felt nauseous. I could barely pray. Besides my children, the only thing that gave me strength to get out of bed was praise.

I kept a CD by Pastor Isaac Pitre playing in my room. He and his wife, Denisha, have always been a blessing in my life. I was often too weak or ill to press in to the Spirit, though I knew there was demonic activity in my home. But as soon as I pressed play, the praise CD changed the atmosphere. The Word of God says God inhabits the praises of His people (Ps. 22:3). To inhabit means to live in or take residence. God lives in our praises to Him, and we know the enemy cannot live in the same place where God dwells.

If you have loved ones in the hospital, it is important to create an atmosphere conducive for healing. Doctors and nurses have been trained to be dispassionate and logical, and they often speak negative reports into the atmosphere simply out of routine. When I visited people in the hospital, I used to praise God quietly. Then I got the revelation that I needed to take authority over the atmosphere. I had to praise God with a voice of triumph.

It isn't always appropriate to shout in a hospital room, but there are times when we need to get loud in our praise The Word of God says after the children of Israel walked around the walls of Jericho seven times, they blew the trumpets; then Joshua commanded them to shout. When the trumpets sounded and the people shouted, the walls fell down, and the Israelites walked right in and took the city (Josh. 6). Triumphant praise brings victory, but it requires a loud sound to permeate the atmosphere. Revelation 5:11–14 says thousands upon ten thousands of angels, living creatures, and elders encircled the throne of God and in a *loud* voice sang, "Worthy is the Lamb, who was slain, to receive power and wealth and wisdom and strength and honor and glory and praise!"

Can you imagine the crowd at the Super Bowl, World Series, or NBA Finals just watching the game in silence? No way! Whether for points scored, a great play made, or someone shooting a T-shirt into the stands, sports fans find a reason to be vocal. That's the type of attitude we should have when praising the Lord. We are on the winning team, and nothing should quiet our praise. Get loud celebrating the King of kings.

Again we see in Revelation 19:6–8 that the wedding celebration of the Lamb was so loud it is compared to a roar of rushing waters and loud peals of thunder. Those gathered were shouting, "Hallelujah! For our Lord God Almighty reigns." Both celebrations in Revelation encourage us to look forward to and rejoice in Christ's victory. This loud praise is a way to share in Christ's triumph on the cross (Col. 2:15). It is a way to rejoice in the Lord for what He has already done and will do in the future.

We see in 2 Samuel 6 that David praised God for who He is—for His power and greatness—and for all He has done. His praise was loud and boastful. When we give God boisterous praise, it builds our confidence and allows God to grow larger in our hearts. It shifts our focus from the battle we're fighting to the Lord of the battle, reminding us that He is bigger than any problem or circumstance. Knowing who God is and what He has already done equips us to go into any battle with the voice of triumph. We can join with Christ in advancing His kingdom, knowing He will intervene on our behalf as we proclaim His Word. We can also look forward to the victory celebrations, where we will give thanks to His holy name and triumph in His praise.

GO TO WAR WITH YOUR PRAISE

I hope you can see by now that praise is much more than a song. It is also more than a covering. It is a weapon for us to carry into battle. This type of triumph praise invites God into the situation, intimidates our opponent, and motivates us to move forward in Christ's victory. It puts the enemy on notice and looks forward to God's intervention on behalf of His people. Consider this passage in the Book of Numbers.

> When you go into battle in your own land against an enemy who is oppressing you, sound a blast on the trumpets. Then you will be remembered by the LORD your God and rescued from your

enemies. Also at your times of rejoicing—your appointed feasts and New Moon festivals—you are to sound the trumpets over your burnt offerings and fellowship offerings, and they will be a memorial for you before your God. I am the LORD your God.

—NUMBERS 10:9–10

Praise invites God into the situation. The Scriptures paint a glorious picture of how God is moved through praise. David noted, "I will praise God's name in song and glorify him with thanksgiving. This will please the LORD more than an ox, more than a bull with its horns and hoofs" (Ps. 69:30–31). It pleases God to hear our praise. As I mentioned previously, He inhabits the praises of His people (Ps. 22:3). That's how much He loves it when we praise Him.

The Bible says, "Submit yourselves, then, to God. Resist the devil, and he will flee from you. Come near to God and he will come near to you" (James 4:7–8). God is not only pleased by praise, but He is also drawn nearer to us because of it. That is why it is so critical that our praises be lifted to God not just when things are going well but also in times of lack, trouble, confusion, and fear—so He can truly be our "refuge in time of distress" (Jer. 16:19).

God will deliver us if we simply call out to Him. Psalm 9:2–3 says, "I will be glad and rejoice in You; I will sing praise to Your name, O Most High. When my enemies turn back, they shall fall and perish at Your presence" (NKJV). And again the psalmist says, "I will call upon the LORD, who is worthy to be praised; so shall I be saved from my enemies" (Ps. 18:3, NKJV). Praise brings deliverance and victory. As we praise Him, we declare His power and might, and God responds by doing what only He can. Consider these examples of how God brought victory through praise.

> After consulting the people, Jehoshaphat appointed men to sing to the LORD and to praise him for the splendor of his holiness as they went out at the head of the army, saying: "Give thanks to the LORD, for his love endures forever." As they began to sing and praise, the LORD set ambushes against the men of Ammon and Moab and Mount Seir who were invading Judah, and they were

defeated....Then, led by Jehoshaphat, all the men of Judah and Jerusalem returned joyfully to Jerusalem, for the LORD had given them cause to rejoice over their enemies.

—2 CHRONICLES 20:21–22, 27

The voice of the LORD will shatter Assyria; with his scepter he will strike them down. Every stroke the LORD lays on them with his punishing rod will be to the music of tambourines and harps, as he fights them in battle with the blows of his arm.

—ISAIAH 30:31–32

When the trumpets sounded, the people shouted, and at the sound of the trumpet, when the people gave a loud shout, the wall [Jericho] collapsed; so every man charged straight in, and they took the city.

—JOSHUA 6:20

Upon receiving such orders, he put them in the inner cell and fastened their feet in the stocks. About midnight Paul and Silas were praying and singing hymns to God, and the other prisoners were listening to them. Suddenly there was such a violent earthquake that the foundations of the prison were shaken. At once all the prison doors flew open, and everybody's chains came loose.

—ACTS 16:24–26

You are my hiding place; you will protect me from trouble and surround me with songs of deliverance.

—PSALM 32:7

PRAISE IS A WEAPON FOR SPIRITUAL WARFARE

Praise destroys yokes and breaks the back of the enemy. That is why the Bible says, "Let the high praises of God be in their mouth, and a two-edged sword in their hand; to execute vengeance upon the heathen, and punishments on the peoples" (Ps. 149:6–7, KJV). Praise will drive out the enemy. First Samuel 16:23 says whenever an evil spirit attacked King Saul, David would play his harp. "Then relief would come to Saul; he would feel better, and the evil spirit would leave him."

Praise silences the enemy. The Bible says in Psalm 8:2, "From the lips of children and infants you have ordained praise because of your enemies, to silence the foe and the avenger." Praise also counters the spirit of despair. Isaiah 61:3 says God gives those who grieve "a crown of beauty instead of ashes, the oil of gladness instead of mourning, and a garment of praise instead of a spirit of despair. They will be called oaks of righteousness, a planting of the LORD for the display of his splendor."

The Hebrew word for this kind of warfare praise is *halal*. It means to make a show or rave about, to glory in or boast upon, to be clamorously foolish about your adoration of God.[5] The Bible instructs us to praise Him with a dance and many instruments.

I thank God that He always leads us in triumph in Christ and through us diffuses the fragrance of His knowledge in every place (2 Cor. 2:14). I pray that the Lord will help each of us praise Him with the voice of triumph. I thank Him for the victory we have in Christ's death on the cross and the victory we will share when He returns in glory. I pray that each person reading this will give thanks to His holy name and triumph in His praise.

In the midst of tragedy and failure, we are able to give God the praise because we know He is still good. Our circumstances never change the greatness of the immutable God, who is the same yesterday, today, and forevermore. Even in his sorrow the psalmist said, "I will yet praise him" (Ps. 43:5). I pray that becomes your testimony too—that you will praise God regardless of your circumstance.

I looked in amazement one Sunday as a young father praised the Lord at the altar with tears streaming down his face. He had just buried his fourteen-year-old son the week prior, yet he chose to praise and worship almighty God. How could he do that? The question is, how could he not? If we are devastated by life's trials, our peace and strength can come only from God.

When we praise God, we magnify Him. So the more we praise God, the bigger He becomes. The bigger God becomes, the smaller our devastation becomes. So put on your garment of praise, and never leave home without it.

JOY COMES
IN THE MORNING

I remember sitting on my bed in the home I'd just moved to, thinking, "It's official." The divorce was not final, but I could sense that the marriage was over. I felt completely uncovered. The new home had no window treatments yet, so as night fell, the darkness encroached into our home. I felt a similar darkness invading my heart. My children and I were now on our own to make do with what we had. How would I make it alone? My husband was all I had known. Darkness continued to fill our house, still cluttered with unpacked boxes. Like a child I wanted to sleep with a night-light.

As it grew darker outside, it seemed to grow darker in my heart. I recall inviting all the children to come sleep in Mommy's room. Unfortunately they had grown out of that stage and basically looked at me as if I were crazy. They were each used to sleeping alone; I was not. I kept the television and the lights on all night to drive away the dark loneliness. I started laughing when I thought of the lyrics of Bobby Womack's song "If You Think You're Lonely Now." Yep, loneliness is definitely worse at night. *Thanks*, Bobby.

Death, financial collapse, and betrayal can leave us feeling lonely in heart and mind. As a result, reality can become hard to discern, heightening feelings of uncertainty, especially at night. In the night the world grows quiet, and time seems to slow. It is when you come face-to-face with your thoughts and hurts. In the night friends and family are not easily accessible. Spirits of discouragement and depression flourish as fear tightens its grip.

I had to learn how to maneuver through the night alone. My bed was no longer a place of rest, comfort, and love. Night became agonizing, even unbearable. I developed more compassion for those who turn to alcohol, promiscuity, or prescription drugs to deal with crisis. I thank God for Christ; He became my sword and shield. When I finally stopped crying, I developed a different kind of closeness to my Master, and He gave me comfort and peace.

The transformative lesson God taught me in that dark hour is that the morning will come when you learn how to endure the night. To endure means to suffer or tolerate.[1] I didn't want to suffer or tolerate the night, but that only delayed my morning.

IN THE STILL OF THE NIGHT

What is expected of you in the night season? Israel had been through a very tumultuous season when God spoke in Hosea 14:5 and said, "I will be as the dew unto Israel" (KJV). This little verse is packed with revelation. Dew is the tiny drops of moisture that appear on cool surfaces in the early morning. We often see it glistening on plants and blades of grass on clear days. But as my mom would say, "What does that have to do with the price of coffee?" I'm glad you asked.

Dew is usually produced late at night or early in the morning before the sun rises. It brings relief to vegetation and livestock by providing water to sustain them when the sun is the hottest. Even when rain is scarce, it is possible for dew to form before the sun comes up. In the same way, it is the dew formed in the night season that will nourish your soul and sustain you in the heat of your trial. This supernatural dew will give you everything you need.

The dew point is the temperature at which moisture in the air begins to condense. Objects receive heat from the sun during the day, but when night comes, the blade of grass is not able to retain the heat that has been stored. So it becomes cool, as does the air around it. When the air reaches the dew point, it can no longer hold all the moisture present, and the excess is deposited as dew on the grass and plants.[2]

Natural dew can be produced only when everything is still; the process occurs in the quiet of the night. Likewise God wants to produce something in our lives during the stillness of the night season. Before the day starts, God is waiting for us. He wants our attention on Him and Him alone. When we wait in His presence, God will begin to nourish us.

Dew doesn't collect when it's windy. Dew doesn't appear during rainstorms. It doesn't form when the air is hot. Dew forms when things are cool and still. Before your joy comes in the morning, you must have a season of God-filled quietness when you can hear His voice. Isaiah 30:15 says we shall receive strength "in quietness and in confidence" (KJV). You can't get clear direction when there is commotion; the noise in your environment frustrates communication. Rather in stillness the voice of God can be clearly heard.

In the darkest of night the enemy will torment your mind. He will make you restless and agitated. My heart was broken over and over during my transition process, and I was still wincing from spiritual wounds I suffered. On many nights I would drive for hours on end. My mind would not rest, and I had no peace. It was extremely difficult for me to get nourishment from the Lord. I was not still enough to hear His voice.

I constantly wanted to tell friends and family how awful my situation was. I couldn't hear God over the commotion of my complaints. I needed the beauty of a meek a quiet spirit (1 Pet. 3:4); I needed to "study to be quiet" (KJV), as the Bible admonishes in 1 Thessalonians 4:11.

It wasn't until I got the mind of Christ and shut my mouth that God was able to intervene. He comforted me and held me in His arms. I felt the Holy Spirit envelop me. His presence sustained me when I stopped seeking vindication. I heard the Lord say, "Hold your peace, and I will fight your battle." As I rested in His bosom, I felt supernatural peace and renewed strength. The dew of the Lord formed in the night season, and joy awaited me in the morning.

STRENGTH IN THE NIGHT SEASON

The dew that comes in the night season gives us the power to overcome. We read in Deuteronomy 33:28–29: "Then Israel shall dwell in safety, the fountain of Jacob alone, in a land of grain and new wine; His heavens shall also drop dew. Happy are you, O Israel! Who is like you, a people saved by the LORD, the shield of your help and the sword of your majesty! Your enemies shall submit to you, and you shall tread down their high places" (NKJV).

There is a correlation between the dew God releases in our season of hardship and His power and strength. The Holy Spirit gives us the power to defeat the enemy. No matter what the devil has planned, those who have been anointed by this heavenly dew have the power to conquer all the high places of the enemy.[3]

During my season of famine—when I did not have the finances, friends, or faith I used to have—my night season became even darker. But ironically this is when God blessed me. He poured life into my spirit and touched my soul. Everything I wanted my husband to do, God did. Although heartache still remained, the hopelessness began to leave.

Only God could have performed the intricate surgery I needed to restore my broken heart. I began to learn how to walk and talk again. I was a little wobbly in the Spirit, but God held my hand during His spiritual rehabilitation period. In the place of quietness He filled me with strength. As Psalm 118:14 says, "The LORD is my strength and song, and is become my salvation" (KJV).

THE DEW BRINGS FAVOR AND BLESSING

Proverbs 19:12 says the king's wrath is like the roaring of a lion, but his favor "is like the dew on the grass" (NKJV). You probably know the favor of God is sweet. Without the dew season, you fit right into the crowd.

But when God sends His dew, it comes with an increase of favor. The Lord will command blessings to overtake you.

Matthew 24:45 says, "Who then is a faithful and wise servant, whom his lord hath made ruler over his household, to give them meat in due season?" (KJV). If you stay faithful over the little, God promises to make you ruler over much. Waiting on the promises of God in the night season can be difficult; sometimes it may look as though life is passing you by. You may even be tempted to manipulate people to move in your best interest. But God says that is not necessary. Just be faithful over what He has given you, and you *will* be blessed!

Many women who were abandoned in ministry use social media to plead their case and win the support of as many church members as possible. Unfortunately when they do this, they run the risk of splitting the ministry and bringing reproach on the Lord—all because they fear losing everything. I understand that temptation. I wasn't just afraid; I was *terrified* that I was going to lose everything. And guess what? I did lose everything. Thank God I did, because most of the things I lost were contaminated.

I remained faithful over the little I had. What does it profit a man to gain the entire world and lose his soul? If you are willing to release what you have in obedience to God, He will restore. God has proven Himself true to His Word. He is restoring everything the enemy stole. This time around is better because there is liberty and joy. Don't allow the enemy to confuse you with fear in your night season. Be obedient, for your morning is nigh.

THE DEW BRINGS PROVISION

In Genesis 27 Isaac prayed a powerful blessing over his son Jacob. He said, "Therefore may God give you of the dew of heaven, of the fatness of the earth, and plenty of grain and wine. Let peoples serve you, and nations bow down to you. Be master over your brethren, and let your mother's sons bow down to you. Cursed be everyone who curses you, and blessed be those who bless you" (Gen. 27:28–29, NKJV). That passage is actually speaking of provision; God was promising to give Jacob all he needed and more.

As you know, God provided manna for the children of Israel while they were wandering in the wilderness. In the mornings, the camp would be wet with dew, and when it evaporated, flaky manna would be left (Exod. 16). The manna fell early in the morning, and it fell upon the dew (Num. 11:9). In the same way, God's provision comes with His dew anointing.

Most grazing animals feed early in the morning to drink in the dew, which is able to sustain them through the heat of the day. The dew is able to sustain vegetation as well. In the wilderness, the manna that was left when the dew dissipated sustained the people of Israel until they reached their promised land.

In order to receive the manna, they had to rise each morning and gather what was left when the dew evaporated. When we are walking through our wilderness, our dry and thirsty land, God will sustain us with His presence, the refreshing touch of His hand, or a word that will enlighten or encourage. This dew buoys us until the rain comes!

THE JOY OF THE LORD

"Seek the Lord while He may be found, call upon Him while He is near" (Isa. 55:6, NKJV). If the Lord tells us to seek Him while He may be found, then there must be a time when He cannot be found. The dew season is not permanent. You may be thinking, "Hey, you just got me excited about the dew of God, and now you're telling me it won't last?" Yes. Don't miss your moment with God. Seasons are temporary. The summer does not last all year. Neither does the dew season.

There will be times in your life when you will not receive the same nourishment from God that you did during a previous season. My time with God now is different than the way it was when I was going through my transition. If I had missed that dew season during my transition, I would not be sustained by His joy today.

Do you have the joy of the Lord? Joy has been described as the evidence of God's presence in a person's life. If God is in your life, if you are filled with the Spirit of God, then this fruit of the Spirit will be apparent in your life. Now please don't mistake happiness for joy. It's easy to do that. The New International Version mentions "joy" or "rejoicing" nearly two hundred fifty times, but it mentions "happiness" only six times.[4] Happiness depends upon what happens to you. It is reliant on your circumstances. Joy is lasting because it is dependent on God's goodness. You need all the outside conditions to be right in order to be happy. But joy comes from inside.

One morning I woke up, and I felt different. I looked in the mirror and didn't see a face that was wracked with pain and anguish. I had a glow, and a smile rested on my lips. What was going on? I didn't have the weird pains in my chest and stomach. I actually felt an unusual and very unnatural strength beginning to rise up in me. What was this? Had joy finally arrived at my address? Yes joy was here, and it was accompanied by strength.

I endured an extremely long night season. There were times when I thought life was over. I had no idea whether I could feel joy again. But when the morning came, my outlook was different. I felt the warmth of joy's presence on my face. I felt like the five virgins who had oil in their lamps and were ready to meet the bridegroom (Matt. 25:1–13). I was not like the five virgins who did not have oil and were not ready when their bridegroom arrived. I was not living in regret. I was living in joy. Everything I endured in the night season prepared me to partake of the joy that came in the morning. That joy is indescribable.

Once you have joy, refuse to let the enemy take it from you. Sometimes we're robbed of our joy. You may have endured a divorce and now feel you're inferior in the sight of God. Or you may have had a brush with the law and feel you're not welcome in God's house. Maybe you feel people would not understand if they knew the secrets of your past. Countless men and women cannot forgive themselves, and as a result they lose their joy unnecessarily. When the enemy dredges up your past, make sure you remind him of his future.

Let's look at a perfect example of joy: Jesus. The night before He was betrayed, Jesus told His disciples, "These things have I spoken unto you, that my joy might remain in you, and that your joy might be full" (John 15:11, KJV). On the last night of His life, while facing a crucible unlike any other in history, Jesus spoke about love and joy. And the next day He willingly went to the cross and died for us.

The writer of Hebrews looks back on Jesus's attitude in light of His sacrifice and writes these words: "Let us fix our eyes on Jesus, the author and perfecter of our faith, who for the joy set before him endured the cross, scorning its shame" (Heb. 12:2). Do you want to know why the writer of Hebrews says Jesus endured the cross, scorning its shame, because of the joy that was set before Him? Do you want to know why the cross was an object of joy for Jesus? Here's why: Jesus didn't suffer on the cross for Himself; He did it for us. There's joy even in a cross when you're bearing it for someone else.

Philippians 4:4 says, "Rejoice in the Lord always: and again I say, Rejoice" (KJV). Then two verses later we are told to care for (worry about) nothing, thus implying that joy in the Lord is one of the best preparations for the trials of this life. The cure for care is joy in the Lord—and not only joy, but joy over again, "re-joy." You know the prefix "re" usually signifies the duplication of a thing. We are to joy, and then we are to re-joy—"*rejoice!*" Joy is a delightful thing. You can never have too much.

I have heard countless testimonies from people who endured infidelity, the death of a spouse or child, miscarriages, financial ruin, ministry splits, and so much more. Hearing these testimonies encouraged me, not because I learned how many other people had gone through trials, but because I saw that they came out of them successfully. I could rejoice because I understood that God would do it for me too.

When I was in the night season, I used to sing a song as I waited for the morning to finally come. It simply said, "Like the dew in the morning, gently rest upon my heart."[5] The joy that comes in the morning brings new life. This joy is not fleeting. It is strong and stable. Although your circumstances may still be undulating, this joy you'll have the world can't take away.

After I passed through the night season, God engulfed me with His love, joy, and blessings. The joy of the Lord gave me strength to care for my children, pray for my ex-husband, pastor a thriving church, cohost television and radio shows, and maintain my business. I remember when I didn't have strength to pick up a fork and eat. Now I draw from the strength of the Most High and press forward in my purpose and destiny. The joy of the Lord that came in the morning truly became my strength.

CHAPTER
11

BEAUTY
FOR ASHES

My heart was filled with joy as my eyes welled with tears. I sat on the front row of the church and listened to members testify of how God had delivered them from alternative lifestyles, torment, brokenness, and abuse. The fire that once consumed left them covered in ashes. But my beautiful Jesus took the ashes of sorrow, disappointment, and dysfunction that once labeled them as unworthy and hopeless and bestowed upon them beauty instead. They are beautiful in Him because His beauty makes them beautiful.

Like the woman at the well, these precious saints are not afraid to tell everyone to come see a man who can change their life and, as Isaiah 61:3 says, give them "beauty for ashes, the oil of joy for mourning, the garment of praise for the spirit of heaviness; that they might be called trees of righteousness, the planting of the LORD, that he might be glorified" (KJV). The New International Version says God gives "a crown of beauty instead of ashes."

God's beauty does not discriminate. He distributes His beauty to the repentant backslider and to the faithful believer who is experiencing trials. Because of this divine exchange of God's beauty for ashes, those who experience trauma in their lives and actually live to tell their stories find a peace that grounds them and keeps them stable throughout their lives. They don't focus on trivial things.

I cannot count the times people have said, "You're different." What they see in me is nothing I created on my own. The anointing produced in the valley season brings a supernatural beauty that's virtually inexplicable. I have a new confidence and strength that I did not have before. I no longer wear grave clothes and walk in defeat. In the words of the prophet Nehemiah, the joy of the Lord is my strength (Neh. 8:10).

Ashes are what remain after something is burned or destroyed. Most people have gone through the fire at one time or another. Those trials may have all but destroyed them, leaving the residue or ashes of those fiery tribulations on their lives. The apostle Paul is such a one. His life was no cakewalk. He experienced unimaginable hardship for the sake of the gospel; the Bible says Paul even had a thorn in the flesh, which may have been some kind of chronic illness.

If you think you've had problems in life, consider what Paul endured. In his letter to the church at Corinth, he tells of the lashings, beatings, and stoning he received, in addition to the shipwrecks and many days at open sea. Paul said he was generally unwelcome in all areas of the earth. And to top it all off, he said, "All of these trials put together do not compare to the pressure for caring for all of the churches." (See 2 Corinthians 11:28.)

Anytime I get heavy or discouraged about life in general, I read 2 Corinthians 11:22–29, in which Paul describes all the hardships he endured. My problems usually pale in comparison. It is amazing how we complain about the smallest things. We complain about the Internet being down, the weather being too hot or too cold, or the music at church being too loud. Some people even leave the faith over a dispute with another church member. Yet our co-laborers in other nations are being tortured and persecuted for the privilege of being called a Christian, and they don't complain. Instead they count their trials as an honor.

Beloved, we will not always be able to avoid life's fiery trials. It will be necessary for those around us to see the residue of ashes upon us.

We see this clearly in the Book of Daniel when Shadrach, Meshach, and Abednego were thrown into the fiery furnace because they refused to bow down to King Nebuchadnezzar's golden image. But instead of being consumed in the blazing fire—which was so hot it killed the guards who threw the men inside—they could be seen walking around, unbound and unharmed. And there was someone in the furnace with them, a fourth man who looked "like a son of the gods" (Dan. 3:25). Throughout the fiery trial, Jesus never left them.

Shadrach, Meshach, and Abednego trusted God and refused to worship anyone but Him, and God used their situation to display His power. When they came out of the fire unharmed—not a hair on their heads was singed, and they didn't even smell of smoke—the king praised their God, the true and living God. Shadrach, Meshach, and Abednego's test became a witness to the world that their God is all-powerful.

God uses our trials to show His power too. Countless ministers have contacted me expressing their joy that I didn't allow the furnace to stop me. I praise God that my test became a testimony that brings Him glory.

ASHES WILL MAKE US BETTER SERVANTS

In 1 Corinthians 4, Paul calls us "servants," or "stewards" of the mysteries of God (vv. 1–2). In order to be good stewards, we must be found faithful. A steward is a person who manages another's property or financial affairs, one who administers anything as the agent of someone else, a trustee of sorts. What Paul is telling us in 1 Corinthians is that we are to manage the mysteries of God and be found faithful in our position. A steward on an airplane dispenses provisions and attends to the passengers' needs. In much the same way God is calling us to dispense the gospel and care for His flock.

God's assignment is great but not very glamorous. As stewards of the Most High God, we will experience pitfalls and valleys. It comes with the territory. We will be slandered and ostracized. The world hates the believer, so we can expect hardships. Even with all the good they did, both Paul and our Lord Jesus Christ were judged unjustly. We too will go through tribulations and be judged unjustly. But Paul said he didn't concern himself with the judgment of others. He was more concerned about what the Lord thought of him than how people judged him (1 Cor. 4:3–5). We should follow his lead and do the same.

In 1 Corinthians 4, Paul also warns us not to judge others prematurely. The word "judge" in this passage means a strong or vehement expression of disapproval.[1] Paul says not to judge because we don't always know the whole truth. There are some things that only God knows. I learned this the hard way. We all know the verse that says you reap what you sow (Gal. 6:7). Well I reaped a royal harvest of judgment.

Over the years I've seen church scandals, marriage breakups, financial impropriety, and so much more. I would often give my "two cents" in the matter, even though I had no dealings with the parties involved. Then one day I found myself on the other side of that kind of judgment, and I saw just how dangerous it can be. I have heard all kinds of stories about my finances and relationships that are absolutely untrue. This type of judgment can be so damaging to the body of Christ. It causes division and dissension, and it does little to further the healing process. I assure you, I have learned my lesson quite well.

Paul warned us not to judge while he was suffering judgment from leaders of the Corinthian church. They were questioning Paul's leadership as well as his apostleship. Paul set the record straight and let it be known that when Christ judges everyone, "he will bring to light what is hidden in darkness and will expose the motives of men's hearts. At that time each will receive his praise from God" (1 Cor. 4:5). The word translated "praise" in that verse is the Greek word *epainos*.[2] It means approbation or commendation and is used here to describe the praise bestowed upon believers at the judgment seat of Christ. This "praise" from God will be exactly in accordance with each person's actions at the revelation of Jesus Christ.

We must not allow people's judgments to hinder us. The truth will always be exposed. The enemy is a master of deception; that is why things can appear real when they are not. In our persecution and trials we must know that God will reward us for our suffering as long as we remain in Christ.

There is a popular television show called *The Biggest Loser*, where overweight contestants compete to lose weight in hopes of winning thousands of dollars. The constants have personal trainers who push them to their breaking point. The training is grueling and often painful. But in the end the contestants leave with beautiful, healthy bodies. No pain no gain, the saying goes. We may be going through the pain of our lives, but the Lord is our "trainer." He knows what we can bear, and in the end the test will lead us to a life that's new and beautiful.

ASHES FROM SIN

Too many ministry scandals have played out publicly in the media. America has mocked, scoffed, and belittled the leaders involved. We presumed them guilty until they were proven innocent. We must understand that the consequences of sin are very serious. The Bible says the wages of sin is death (Rom. 6:23). This could mean the death of a marriage, lifestyle, family dynamic, ministry, or so much more. Sin has its own recompense. That being said, we do not need to heap more misery upon the fallen leader by assaulting him or her with judgment. Why am I saying this? God reveals what He wants to heal. God loves fallen leaders, and He reveals their sin so they will stop and repent of the ungodly behavior.

Sometimes when a leader falls, Christians think they are showing love when they say, "Don't worry about it. We don't care what you did. We will support you anyway. We are standing by you." This is simply another extreme. These leaders don't need their mistakes glossed over. They need to be held accountable so they can be healed and not fall into that sin again. Revelation 3:19 says God chastises those He loves. It may be painful for them to go through such discipline, but consequences are necessary for deliverance.

What if a fallen leader repents and gets right with God? What if the fallen leader's heart was broken and contrite? What if the fallen leader changed his ways? Then God would restore such a one, and so should we. We must be careful how we talk about fallen leaders. God may be in the process of restoring them. And if He is, then you are coming against God when you come against them. Our judgment should stay within the boundaries of the Word. We follow a leader as he or she follows Christ. We must not walk in judgment based upon our opinion of the situation.

God is able to remove our sins as far as the east is from the west, to be remembered no more (Ps. 103:12). He will cast our past mistakes in the sea of forgetfulness. When you humble yourself in repentance, God replaces the ashes of your sin with beautiful holiness.

The same holds true for those who are injured by someone else's actions. Joseph is a perfect example. He was ostracized and sold into slavery by his brothers, accused by Potiphar's wife of trying to molest her, and thrown into prison. It would have been easy to think Joseph must have done something wrong for so many bad things to happen to him. But Joseph was innocent, and God was with him through it all. He went through the pit experience to make it to the palace. We must not judge what we do not know by the Spirit. We will be judged by the same measure we use to judge others (Matt. 7:2).

ASHES OF GOD'S JUDGMENT

Let's not forget what ash is. It is the residue left after something burns. God is preparing us for the judgment seat of Jesus Christ. He is looking to see what remains after the consuming fires of our trials. The Bible says fire tests the quality of a man's work. Will you be standing on a firm foundation? First Corinthians 3 talks about the kinds of material that can make up our foundation:

> If any man builds on this foundation using gold, silver, costly stones, wood, hay or straw, his work will be shown for what it is, because the Day will bring it to light. It will be revealed with fire, and the fire will test the quality of each man's work. If what he has built survives, he will receive his reward. If it is burned up, he will suffer

loss; he himself will be saved, but only as one escaping through the flames.

—1 Corinthians 3:12–15

This passage is clearly speaking of the judgment seat of Christ, when Jesus will judge all of us who are saved. There are many believers who are not living a sold-out life for Christ. They are planning to enter heaven by the skin of their teeth. God knows there are also many believers living holy and sacrificial lives, who are sold out for Christ and not indulging in the things of this world. Yet both types of Christians will enter heaven. So God in His justice has established the judgment seat of Christ to reward and rank those who will rule and reign with Him. Everything we do in the short time we are on the earth will determine the rewards we receive for eternity.

Paul makes reference to the judgment seat of Christ in 2 Corinthians 5:10 and Romans 14:10. What is this judgment seat of Christ? It comes from the Greek word *bema*.[3] It is a judicial seat, like the one an umpire stands on to declare who won the race—who earned the gold, silver, or bronze medal, and who will go home empty-handed.

So the picture we have is of a race where the winners receive something from the umpire who stands upon his judgment seat, the *bema*. On what will we be judged? First Corinthians 3:12 tells us we will be judged on how we built upon the foundation of Christ. How we build will determine the level of beauty we will receive for our ashes. Unfortunately some believers will not receive any beauty for their ashes. Before we examine the kinds of beauty God exchanges for ashes, let's look at the types of ashes He rejects.

Wood—ashes of good ideas instead of God ideas

Psalm 127:1 says, "Unless the Lord builds the house, its builders labor in vain. Unless the Lord watches over the city, the watchmen stand guard in vain." Wood reminds us of the houses we've built. Though they may be very nice houses, if the Lord didn't build them, our labor was in vain. We can't settle for doing good things; we must do what God called us to do. For instance, donating generously to missions is undeniably good. But if God called you to be a missionary and you chose to give lots of money instead, you have been disobedient, and your benevolence will be burned up like wood.

It seems so many Christians want to make lots of money and have the notoriety of megachurch pastors. But what if you are not called to be a megachurch pastor? What if God has called you to be an evangelist? We must be careful to not walk in our own agenda but in God's will for our lives. Christians who are not in pulpit ministry often do the same thing. They spend their energy trying to make things happen that they were never called to do. Good ideas can be bad ideas when they are not God ideas.

Hay—ashes of unfinished work

Paul told the Galatians, "Ye did run well; who did hinder you that ye should not obey the truth? This persuasion cometh not of him that calleth you" (Gal. 5:7–8, KJV). He was warning them against the danger of unfinished work. Most of us are familiar with hay. It is something farmers feed to animals, and if it is not consumed, little can be done with it. It becomes of almost no value. Hay can stand for the good things we started to do that became of almost no value because we didn't finish them. I am leery of building projects that have been in the works for thirty years yet no ground has been broken. Something is terribly wrong if your church is involved in a building campaign for fifty years. That is unfinished work. We must finish the work God calls us to do and not give in to procrastination. Procrastination can cause us to miss our moment and abort our destiny.

Stubble—ashes of empty works

Stubble are the reeds and stalks left after grain has been harvested. If you've ever seen a cornfield in late autumn, you've seen stubble littering the ground. Stubble, being neither seed nor usable grain, serves very little purpose. It represents the time we wasted doing things that accomplished nothing for God. Empty works are not necessarily sinful deeds. I've met wives totally frustrated with husbands who play video games all day. It is not necessarily sinful to play video games, but this typically does not produce anything of value for the kingdom. There are plenty of Sundays when Christians do absolutely nothing for God. They show up for church, and that's it. God calls that empty works, and no reward will be given.

Now let's look at the different types of beauty you can receive for your ashes.

Gold—the beauty of faith

The Bible says in 1 Peter 1:7, "These trials will show that your faith is genuine. It is being tested as fire tests and purifies gold—though your faith is far more precious than mere gold. So when your faith remains strong through many trials, it will bring you much praise and glory and honor on the day when Jesus Christ is revealed to the whole world" (NLT).

If you want that kind of faith, take careful note of one thing this verse promises: your faith *will* be tried. If you think you have great faith and you haven't been through some trials that tested your faith, then there are two possibilities: either your faith isn't ready for a sore trial, or your time of testing hasn't come yet. Be assured it will. Tests are never anything we can look forward to, but when we come out the other side, our faith will bring praise and honor and glory to Jesus Christ.

If you walk closely with the Lord, He will reveal when your season of trial is about to come. The Lord spoke to me again and again about getting my house in order. I thought perhaps someone was going to die. I kept asking my husband, "Why is God saying get your house in order?" My spirit was grieved, and I remember telling God, "Please, Lord, do not make me go through anything. I promise I will say yes to whatever You want me to do. I do not need to go through any trials." God was showing me that my season of testing was here.

Looking back I can now see why we go through the fire. I am not the same person I used to be. I am better, stronger, and more compassionate—all because the fire purified me, burning away the things that were not like Him. This type of change cannot be taught; it must be experienced.

Silver—the beauty of endurance

"I have fought a good fight, I have finished my course, I have kept the faith" (2 Tim. 4:7, KJV). Just like the silver or gray hair on the heads of the Lord's "seasoned" servants, silver reminds us of faithfulness. Our endurance, our willingness to stay in the faith over the long haul, is very important to God. One of my favorite things in the entire world is to see an elderly couple holding hands. It just makes my heart leap to see a man and woman who have been together for fifty or more years. We know they must have had hard times, but they endured them together. It is not the fastest runner in the race who pleases God, but rather the one who endures until the end.

Trials can be so horrifying you will want to give up. Trials push you out of your comfort zone and right into God's refining fire. God allows this because He wants to see if He can trust you and if you will trust Him. I am amazed at the stamina of our military. During training they are often pushed to the very edge of collapse. That is because their commanding officers need to know they can endure when the battle is most intense. In the same way God is looking for a few good men and women who will not give up in the heat of battle.

Precious stones—the beauty of winning souls

"Then those who feared the LORD talked with each other, and the LORD listened and heard. A scroll of remembrance was written in his presence concerning those who feared the LORD and honored his name. 'They will be mine,' says the LORD Almighty, 'in the day when I make up my treasured possession. I will spare them, just as in compassion a man spares his son who serves him'" (Mal. 3:16–17).

The precious stones represent the fruit you bear for Jesus, especially the souls you bring to Him. Why did we get saved? I hope for most of us it is so we can live eternally with God. What is our assignment on earth? We must bring others into the kingdom of God. He who wins souls is wise (Prov. 11:30). Our focus must not be on amassing riches on earth; it must be on seeing souls saved.

Many churches are being built on entertainment platforms to keep members, well, entertained. If a church draws members through entertainment, it will have to keep members in the same manner. A church should draw souls by the Spirit of the Lord. If the Spirit of the Lord draws the souls, then the Spirit of the Lord will keep them. Souls are beautiful to God. He is not focused on how many members a church has. God is interested in how many souls are being snatched from the pit of hell and delivered from a life of torment.

Wood, hay, and stubble are easily obtained and found in large quantities. Gold, silver, and precious stones are found deep in the earth and are not as easy to acquire. Some people think they will receive a great reward in heaven because they endured heartache and pain while on earth. That has no bearing on the reward they will receive in eternity. We will be judged by Jesus for everything we have done on earth to advance His kingdom. If we are judged to be righteous, Jesus promises us crowns that symbolize our status in eternity.

CROWNS OF BEAUTY

The New International Version translates the phrase "beauty for ashes" in Isaiah 61:3 as a "crown of beauty instead of ashes." Throughout Scripture crowns are worn by those given authority to rule or those who have emerged victorious in a race or battle. The crowns God gives us for our ashes are just as significant. Let's take a look at the crowns of beauty that will be available to us.

The incorruptible crown

"Do you not know that in a race all the runners run, but only one gets the prize? Run in such a way as to get the prize. Everyone who competes in the games goes into strict training. They do it to get a crown that will not last; but we do it to get a crown that will last forever. Therefore I do not run like a man running aimlessly; I do not fight like a man beating the air" (1 Cor. 9:24–26).

The incorruptible crown is the victor's crown. It is worn by those who resist temptation. One of the best feelings in the world is when you have resisted temptation, when, for instance, you walk away from that big piece of chocolate cake that was calling your name. It gives you a feeling of great accomplishment. Your "chocolate cake" may be an ex-boyfriend, overspending, pride, or revenge. No matter what the enemy may use to tempt you, God wants you to follow Jesus's example and resist the temptations of life. You will receive an eternal reward for not giving in to your flesh.

The crown of rejoicing

In 1 Thessalonians Paul mentions a second crown. He says, "For what is our hope, our joy, or the crown in which we will glory in the presence of our Lord Jesus when he comes? Is it not you?" (1 Thess. 2:19). The crown of rejoicing is the soul-winner's crown; it is for those who lead others to Christ. If you were standing at the judgment seat of Christ today and Jesus asked you how many souls you won for His kingdom, what would your answer be? Do you even think about winning souls throughout the day? When I go into public places and see large groups of people, my heart aches because I know many of them have never heard the gospel. We must have a passion for the lost and make it a priority to tell them about Jesus.

The crown of righteousness

"Now there is in store for me the crown of righteousness, which the Lord, the righteous Judge, will award to me on that day—and not only to me, but also to all who have longed for his appearing" (2 Tim. 4:8). The crown of righteousness is for those who love the Lord's return. Pastor Douglas Chukwuemeka is our apostolic covering at Majestic Life Church, and he is so excited about the Lord's return. The only way a person can be excited about Christ's return is if he or she is living holy.

Pastor Doug told me he was once in an elevator on his way to one of his college classes when the power went out. The elevator wasn't stopped for long, and he was able to reach the floor where his class was being held. But he said when the elevator doors opened, the hall was completely dark. He began to scream at the top of his lungs, "I am ready, Jesus! Take me, Lord. I am ready!" He was jumping and screaming with excitement because he thought the rapture was taking place. Just as he finished screaming, the lights came on and everyone was looking at him. Pastor Doug longs for Christ's return, and I believe he will have a crown of righteousness waiting for him.

The crown of glory

"Be shepherds of God's flock that is under your care, serving as overseers—not because you must, but because you are willing, as God wants you to be; not greedy for money, but eager to serve; not lording it over those entrusted to you, but being examples to the flock. And when the Chief Shepherd appears, you will receive the crown of glory that will never fade away" (1 Pet. 5:2–4). The crown of glory is for those who took care of God's flock. Pastors, your reward will be great if you are feeding your flock. Have we forgotten that we are supposed to serve the sheep and not the other way around? God is requiring much more from pastors. Those who are prioritizing money over genuinely ministering to the congregation should beware.

The crown of life

"Do not be afraid of what you are about to suffer. I tell you, the devil will put some of you in prison to test you, and you will suffer persecution for ten days. Be faithful, even to the point of death, and I will give you the crown of life" (Rev. 2:10). The crown of life is for those who suffer and even die for Christ. Tears fill my eyes to know that men, women, and children willingly lay down their lives for the cause of Christ.

All over the world Christians are being martyred for the cause of Christ. Not long ago in Sudan a Christian teenager was beheaded simply for being a believer. Islamic militants had been watching him for months and were able to tell by his lifestyle that he was a follower of Christ.[4] What a testimony. Would someone know you are a Christian just by watching your life each day? That young man, and countless others around the globe, will receive a great reward for being willing to make the ultimate sacrifice to stand for Christ.

In Ruth 2:12, Boaz tells Ruth, "The LORD recompense thy work, and a full reward be given thee of the LORD God of Israel, under whose wings thou art come to trust" (KJV). What will be your full recompense? What reward will be given to you for all you have done for Christ? Remember, only what we do for Christ will last (1 John 2:15–17). Will you receive your crown of beauty?

CHAPTER
12

POWER
FOR PURPOSE

I t always amuses me to watch my youngest son when his birthday is approaching. Months in advance he reminds anyone and everyone who will listen that July 7 is coming. He gets so excited about the prospect of receiving presents and being the center of attention.

When I was younger, I used to get excited about my birthday too. But as I have gotten older, that excitement has all but disappeared. I now view my birthdays as benchmarks in my life, times when I reflect on both my accomplishments and failures.

There was a time when I was the youngest person in the group. I was a junior trustee at our church in North Brentwood, Maryland, when I was twelve years old. When we were students at the University of Maryland–Baltimore County, my sister and I became the youngest people in our church to be ordained deaconesses at the age of nineteen. When I started pastoring at the age of twenty-four, my husband and I were usually the youngest ministers at most gatherings. Now as younger leaders emerge on the scene, they remind me that time is still marching forward, and I must make the most of the time God has given me.

This is what makes class reunions either exhilarating or depressing.

They make us reflect on how much (or how little) we have done with our lives. I sometimes think about my classmates. We went to the same high school and lived in similar neighborhoods. Some of my classmates may have had advantages in certain areas while I had a leg up in other areas, but for the most part we had the same opportunities. Yet we each ended up in different places, with some advancing in their careers and others settling comfortably in the middle of the pack.

I can't help but wonder why this happens, why people who start out in the same place end up so differently. As a pastor I have meditated on this. How can two people with similar backgrounds attend the same church, hear the same Word, and yet end up on two completely different paths? One person will pursue a life of faith, the other faithlessness. Despite my transition in life I am forever grateful to God for giving me the grace to move forward. I have a sense of expectation that good things are ahead and that God wants me to reach higher heights and deeper depths. But what about those who were not able to move forward after a devastating loss? Why weren't they able to keep moving?

What we believe about our abilities and opportunities ultimately determines how successful we become. But success is not measured by how much money or "stuff" a person amasses. I read that nearly 46 percent of women suffer from what is being called the "Bag Lady Syndrome."[1] The sufferers don't fit the stereotype of a homeless woman who carries everything she owns in shopping bags. Most have good salaries and decent savings and investments. Yet these women fear they will wind up broke, forgotten, and destitute.

The survey polled almost two thousand women and found that 90 percent felt financially insecure. Forty-six percent were troubled by a "tremendous fear of becoming a bag lady," and this anxiety actually increased as their incomes rose. Among women with annual incomes of more than $100,000, some 48 percent feared a life of destitution. Lily Tomlin, Gloria Steinem, Shirley MacLaine, and Katie Couric "all admitted to having a bag lady in their anxiety closet," writes MSN money columnist Jay McDonald. They all suffer from the bag lady nightmare.[2]

We all have secret fears we toil against and that toil against us. Fears of losing income, our spouse, or stability can be ever present. And though people have more insecurity about money than anything else, the real problem is not a lack of finances but rather a lack of faith.

When I was at my lowest point, I had very little faith. I often wondered if I had inadvertently done something wrong or whether God was angry with me for some reason I could not discern. I even felt I was no longer significant to God. I thought maybe His love for me was based on His love for my husband. My faith was failing. Looking at me on the outside, most people would not have recognized my fears and insecurities, just as many of us wouldn't think journalist Katie Couric would fear being homeless when she earns millions of dollars each year.[3]

But the fact of the matter is, outwardly you can look as though everything is OK but inwardly be full of fear, doubt, and insecurity. And, as this study shows, making lots of money and being successful do not go hand in hand with security. This is why we should never focus our energy on attaining wealth. When we do, we are not being kingdom-minded. Our focus should always be on fulfilling God's purpose for our lives.

Before my transition in life I had the big house, media presence, and nice things so many people think they crave, but those things did not bring fulfillment. Success isn't measured by the size of a person's bank account or how many high-profile people he knows. A successful person can be someone who makes only $15,000 a year but has no debt, because a successful person is a lender and not a borrower. A successful person may be someone who lives in a two-bedroom home on the wrong side of town but has peace and order in her home. She may not wear designer clothes and jewelry, but she is satisfied and her children are living for the Lord. How many people can say that?

Money, fancy cars, and fine houses don't make a person special. During Jesus's last night with His disciples, He told them, "I will ask the Father, and he will give you another Counselor to be with you forever—the Spirit of truth. The world cannot accept him, because it neither sees him nor knows him. But you know him, for he lives with you and will be in you" (John 14:16–17). Jesus sent the Holy Spirit to abide within us. We might seem ordinary on the outside, but there is something extraordinary on the inside. As believers we are not average; beneath the surface we are really queens and kings, a royal priesthood.

A jewel is never recognized in its early stages. It's not until it has been put under pressure that its formation becomes spectacular. In the body of Christ there are countless diamonds in the rough who go unnoticed, unappreciated, and often unloved. It's human nature for people to flock to those with notoriety and wealth. Yet God is attracted to those who are genuine and humble. God sees what others cannot. God recognizes the jewel inside each and every one of us. First Samuel 16:7 reminds us that man looks on the outward appearance, but God looks at the heart.

For the longest time I did not recognize what was inside of me. I saw the strength and boldness in others, but for some reason I could not see it in me. It's like looking at pictures from your twenties and marveling at how beautiful or handsome you were, even though you may not have seen yourself that way at the time. The same is the case with us spiritually. Too often we compare ourselves to others, not realizing we are just as valuable to God as anyone else.

Enduring the uncomfortable pressure of lack caused me to tap into my inner, God-given strength. I was able to draw from a well that overflowed with resources. To my amazement, what I needed was there all the time; it took the pressure of life to prime the pump of my inner well and help me see it. I needed faith to see what God had placed in me. Without faith and the power of the Holy Spirit, we are blind. I praise God that He knows how to uniquely develop each of us for His purpose.

We look to others to mentor us, encourage us, and speak life into us. The only problem is the very people we want to do all those things for us are just people themselves. When I was co-pastor of the eight-thousand-member church, I met many well-known ministers and celebrities. Honestly, I never fit in with those folks, probably because I was not comfortable in my own skin. I would often sit back quietly and observe how they interacted with one another. Watching them often made me wonder who they were without the fine clothes and jewelry, the expensive shoes and handbags. Were they happy? Did they have a close relationship with the Lord, or was ministry just a means to a financial end?

I also observed the "groupies" just waiting for their chance to be in the presence of one of these individuals. I saw clearly that the groupies didn't just want to meet these people; they wanted to *be* these people. The Bible is clear about this. It says: "Keep your lives free from the love of money and be content with what you have, because God has said, 'Never will I leave you; never will I forsake you.' So we say with confidence, 'The Lord is my helper; I will not be afraid. What can man do to me?'" (Heb. 13:5–6).

No one can be a better you, so what good would it do for you to be someone else? We lose our sense of purpose when we try to attain someone else's dream. What has God told *you* to do? Our time on earth is short, especially in light of eternity.

I am reminded of a scene in the movie *Love and Basketball*. The main character, Monica, heaves up a three-point shot. As the ball travels through the air, she stands still for a moment to watch it swish into the basket. But after the ball goes through the net, the other team collects it, pushes it up the court, and quickly scores. Monica, caught flat-footed, was not in a position to defend the ball.

That's how many of us are in life. We're reveling in our victories while God is moving forward and waiting for us to catch up. We are not to spend our lives imitating anyone else, coveting another person's blessing, or rehearsing our victories to hide from our failures. We are to keep it moving. Purpose does not stop; it keeps going until everything God has for us is accomplished.

POSSESSING THE LAND OF YOUR PURPOSE

So that I don't live in the past, I view my birthday as an opportunity to conquer and possess new land. With each birthday comes new challenges to be met and exceeded. I see each new year as an adventure waiting to happen, a time to move forward in my purpose. Each year is an opportunity to take new land—a land filled with great potential for victory and failure. God wants all of us to possess the land of our purpose, and He shows us how in His Word. Look with me at Deuteronomy 11:10–12:

> The land you are entering to take over is not like the land of Egypt, from which you have come, where you planted your seed and irrigated it by foot as in a vegetable garden. But the land you are crossing the Jordan to take possession of is a land of mountains and valleys that drinks rain from heaven. It is a land the LORD your God cares for; the eyes of the LORD your God are continually on it from the beginning of the year to its end.

This passage is packed with revelation, but there are two points I want you to remember: the land of our purpose will not just be handed to us, and possessing the land has nothing to do with who we are, but everything with who God is in us. Let's look more closely at this passage so we can take hold of the purpose God has for us.

We must take the land

God has many blessings in store for us, but He doesn't always hand them to us. There are times when we need to arrest them. Caleb and Joshua saw the Promised Land full of milk, honey, and massive grapes, among other things. The blessings were definitely there, but the men sent with them to scout out the land were afraid to go in and get them (Num. 13–14).

We miss out on blessings every day because we get comfortable with the familiar. So many people exist but never really live because they feel as though they must stay in that restrictive box called comfort. Getting people out of their comfort zones is like trying to drive a car with the emergency brake engaged. Sure, they *can* move, but they have placed something in their own way that keeps them from going forward. Trusting God can be uncomfortable, but He doesn't want us to live in a box. He doesn't want us to miss the land of opportunity year after year by not seizing the opportunity to possess it.

We must desire the land

Possessing the land begins with desire. We must *want* to fulfill God's purpose for our lives. We must want all He has for us. The Bible admonishes us to be content (Phil. 4:12; 1 Tim. 6:6, 8), but we should never become complacent. We should always reach for higher heights. If we limit ourselves, we will never accomplish all God has for us to do. A ministry of a hundred people is wonderful, but if the congregation gets comfortable and stops pressing forward, it may miss its purpose to grow to a thousand members. We must desire to keep moving from glory to glory (2 Cor. 3:18).

When I was in the process of healing after my marriage ended, I was lost and bewildered. I needed God's GPS to put me back on the road to my purpose. I had absolutely no desire to be in ministry again. Through the years I had seen so much hypocrisy, so many ministers who were chasing the almighty dollar instead of serving almighty God, I was fed up and wanted nothing to do with that. So when God began to show me the land of my purpose, a land that included preaching and pastoring, I didn't want to possess it.

I laced up my track shoes, did some stretches, and, like Jonah, was ready to run full speed away from my destiny. God was calling me to do the last thing I wanted to do. But my love for Him inspired me to be obedient despite my lack of desire. And a funny thing happened. When I began to walk in obedience to God, my desire began to change, and my passion for ministry was restored.

We must have faith

In the early 1990s I attended a nondenominational church for the first time. I heard people talk about possessing the land and believing God to meet their physical needs. There was a great attitude of militant faith. We need a strong faith to possess all God has for us. The key is to remember we are only vehicles for God's promises to manifest on the earth, and we must be good stewards of the possessions He gives us. Everything, after all, belongs to the Lord and is His to give as He wishes.

It really has gotten twisted in the kingdom of God to see people who possess the promises of God becoming celebrities to the people of God. When did the church start worshiping the preacher for doing what God told him to do? It is almost pagan. There are many ministries that could have reached higher levels in the kingdom if they had not forgotten that their purpose was not to fulfill their desires but God's.

I have learned that it is very possible to miss your moment. I praise God that He is a God of second, third, and fourth chances. However, there are moments in life that we will never get back and will always regret not taking advantage of. Possessing the land by faith means everything will not be perfect. You may not have all the manpower, money, or time you need, but as long as you have the faith, it will work.

God instructed me to look for a building. The volunteer team that was working closely with me could not understand how we could look for a building when we had no money. Truthfully, I didn't know either. But it wasn't for me to know; it was in God's hands.

God, in His sovereign power, worked all things together for our good. I believe if we had not moved in that moment, we would have delayed our destiny. The children of Israel missed their moment because of doubt and unbelief, and they spent forty years wandering in the wilderness. They could not get Egypt out of their belief system, and they could not see beyond where they were. We must not repeat their mistake. We must step out of the slave mentality, be willing to leave the familiar, and move into the kingdom of more than enough by faith.

DON'T MISS YOUR MOMENT

One of my favorite stories in the Bible is the account of Abigail in 1 Samuel 25. Abigail is the epitome of a woman who did not miss her moment. Abigail was a woman of wisdom and grace, but she was married to a fool named Nabal. His name literally means fool. Abigail is a perfect example of how joining yourself to the wrong person or thing can harm your life.

David and his mighty men protected Nabal's sheepherders from vandals and wild beasts. In return David requested food and drink. Nabal, in a drunken state, refused David's request. When David heard this, he sought to kill everything and everyone connected to Nabal's house. This is when Abigail intervened.

She appeased David first by giving him an abundance of gifts, food, and provisions. She also prophesied over him and admonished him not to damage his integrity as the future king of Israel by shedding innocent, albeit foolish, blood. David was grateful to Abigail for her wisdom. The Word of God says once Nabal sobered up and realized what had happened, his heart died within him, and he became as a stone. Then ten days later the Lord smote Nabal, and he died. Afterward David, recognizing her value, took Abigail as his wife.

Don't miss your moment. Though it seems as though your enemies are prospering, it is just a matter of time before God deals with them. Even if you are married to a fool, God will take care of you.

PURPOSE IS A LAND OF VARIED EXPERIENCES

We read in Deuteronomy 8:7 that the land of promise was "a land with streams and pools of water, with springs flowing in the valleys and hills." When I think of hills and valleys, I think of life's ups and downs. When I was in grade school, my mother took my sister and me to church every Sunday. On the way we would listen to gospel music on the radio. I remember hearing James Cleveland sing "I Don't Feel No Ways Tired." I love the way it describes the journey of a Christian: "Nobody told me that the road would be easy / I don't believe He brought me this far to leave me."[4] This is so true. I often say if God brought you to it, He will take you through it.

All of us will experience mountain and valley experiences, but God promises to be with us through them all. When we truly study the Word of God, we find that God's people, even the heroes of faith, overcame a variety of opposition. Why do we assume our journey will be without struggle?

I now understand that my purpose in God was not contingent on my husband. Hear my heart: I believe in the sanctity of marriage. I believe the marriage covenant is most important to God and that divorce is only allowable as a result of infidelity, physical abuse, or abandonment. When we look at Abigail, God obviously got involved in her situation and dealt with Nabal. I believe God will do the same with us.

But my journey in my marriage and ministry taught me a lot. Now I see that I did not accomplish quite a few things that are necessary for me to fulfill my purpose. I believe God has me on a fast track to redeem the time and complete the work He began in my life.

God called me to pastor, lead, and preach; to start my own businesses and have a media presence. I never walked in the fullness of my purpose due to my own struggles with rejection. God does not give us a cheat sheet when He gives us a test. We either pass or fail. But I am determined to fulfill my purpose and destiny.

In Deuteronomy 11, we read that the Promised Land "is not like the land of Egypt, from which you have come, where you planted your seed and irrigated it by foot as in a vegetable garden" (v. 10). In Egypt the Nile River was the only source of water. The farmers would build trenches and fill them with water. At the end of each trench they made a small dam out of dirt. When it was time to irrigate the vegetation, the farmers would kick down the dam to release the water. This is what life is without Jesus—a lot of working in your own strength to make things happen. When you are in God's purpose for your life, the grace of God gives you the ability to do all things through Christ who strengthens you.

Deuteronomy 11 goes on to say that the land Israel would possess "is a land of mountains and valleys that drinks rain from heaven" (v. 11). God said the land would be fed by rain from heaven. That means whether we are high atop a mountain or trudging through the valley, God's rain will not only reach us, but it will also sustain us. God will take care of us no matter where we are in the journey.

This passage is very significant. It is critical for us to understand that when we are in purpose, God will provide. I remember at one time being fearfully concerned with how I was going to pay my mortgage, often having panic attacks. When the provision I was expecting to receive didn't come through, I can testify that the rain of heaven supplied my needs. I didn't have more than enough, but I had exactly what I needed, and I am grateful for God's goodness. I tell people all over this nation that God is a provider and a keeper if you want to be kept. When you are walking in His purpose and in obedience to His Word, God will take care of you.

GOD IS CONCERNED ABOUT YOU

I often hear people who backslid or found God later in life share their testimonies. They commonly say, "I see now that the hand of God was on my life even when I did not know Him." Sometimes it is difficult to comprehend what it means to serve an infinite God. How can He keep track of each one of us at all times? My mortal mind cannot grasp the magnitude of God's ability. However, I do know His love is real, and it has overwhelmed me many times.

Deuteronomy 11:12 says the land of promise is "a land the LORD your God cares for"; His eyes "are continually on it from the beginning of the year to its end." The Word of God tells us that even when we are in purpose we will face trials (1 Pet. 4:12). We shouldn't be surprised when the enemy attacks. If I were playing football, my objective would be to score a touchdown, and the opposing team would do everything in their power to stop me. Well, the enemy is the same way. He wants to do everything in his power to keep us from walking in our purpose and scoring a victory for the kingdom.

Because we are on God's team, we know we will win, but that doesn't mean we won't incur a few battle wounds in the process. Yet through the highs and lows, the mountains and valleys, we can know that God sees what we endure, and He cares. When you sacrifice and think no one knows or cares, consider this passage in Deuteronomy. God's eyes are always upon you. He knows, and He surely cares. This is why it is imperative that you not compare yourself to others. The fact that someone may be receiving the accolades of man in no way means he is getting the accolades of God.

FIGHT FOR YOUR PURPOSE

The children of Israel wandered in the wilderness for forty years, and by the end of that period the elderly had died off, and only their sons and daughters were left to enter the Promised Land. I am sure they felt great anticipation as they traveled to the land of promise, which was flowing with milk and honey. Yet there were five young women whose anticipation quickly turned to frustration. These women, known as the daughters of Zelophehad, were devastated at the news that they would not be able to receive their portion of the Promised Land. The girls' father had died, and they had no brothers or uncles to inherit the property. The law stated that only males could receive the inheritance.

The traditions of men can bring about death rather than life. The traditions of men can sabotage purpose if we let them. The Bible says Jesus could not do many miracles in some places because of the traditions of men. In Mark 7 Jesus chided the Pharisees for rejecting God's commands in order to keep their traditions. He said in doing this, they made the Word of God of none effect (vv. 9, 13).

Traditions are satanic when they hinder the manifestation of the Word of the Lord. God will never contradict Scripture, but His ways are not our ways, and He wants to do new things in our lives and our churches. He says in Isaiah 43:19, "Behold, I will do a new thing" (KJV). Follow the Spirit of God to keep your purpose alive.

In order to possess the land God has promised us, we must be determined. God does not force His blessing upon us. You can't think your blessings will come just because you received Jesus Christ as your Savior and go to church. Matthew 11:12 says, "The kingdom of heaven suffereth violence, and the violent take it by force" (KJV). God has blessings waiting for us; we just have to take them. The limits are never on God's side; they are always on ours.

The daughters of Zelophehad fought for what was theirs. They decided to talk with the top man himself, Moses. This was not common, considering that women did not have much status in that day. The way you actualize determination is to realize that the promise is not according to merit but according to grace. God did not ask the Israelites to earn the land of Canaan; He gave it to them. It was not contingent on the fruit of their labor but rather upon the grace that was available to them. The same is true for us. Because of God's grace, not our own efforts, we have all we need to possess the promise (Rom. 8:32; Heb. 4:15–16).

But what do we do when we present ourselves to God and ask Him to do something, but nothing happens? Often we become discouraged after about a week. What is the problem? We have not yet understood that God tests us by delaying His answers to our prayers. The daughters of Zelophehad did not get what they wanted when they approached Moses. He did not give them an inheritance in the land; he gave them the promise of an inheritance when they reached the Promised Land. He did not say yes to their request. They had to wait and wait and wait for the actual inheritance. That is what God does to us; He delays the promise to teach us to trust Him.

But the promise is worth fighting for. It is the promise of power, blessing, refreshing, and fruitfulness (Eph. 1:3). It is the promise of becoming the people we always longed to be. The promise is worth fighting for; it is worth the perseverance. Zelophehad's daughters fought for their inheritance, and God answered them.

> So Moses brought their case before the LORD and the LORD said to him, "What Zelophehad's daughters are saying is right. You must certainly give them property as an inheritance among their father's relatives and turn their father's inheritance over to them. Say to the Israelites, 'If a man dies and leaves no son, turn his inheritance over to his daughter. If he has no daughter, give his inheritance to his brothers. If he has no brothers, give his inheritance to his father's brothers. If his father had no brothers, give his inheritance to the nearest relative in his clan, that he may possess it. This is to be a legal requirement for the Israelites, as the LORD commanded Moses.'"
>
> —NUMBERS 27:5–11

Not only did these young women receive their inheritance, but they also won the right for all women to receive inheritances. Because they were determined to possess the land of their purpose, the daughters of Zelophehad were instrumental in the formation of a new law in Israel. When we walk in our purpose we are not only blessed, but we also become a blessing to others. God gives us the grace to influence not only our destiny but also that of future generations. I pray for that grace in my own life. I pray that what I went through will help others avoid the patterns of brokenness that destroy marriages, ministries, finances, and lives.

CHAPTER
13

WHEN HOPE
SEEMS LOST

The sky was remarkably clear August 13, 2011. I was driving alone to church early that Sunday morning, singing softly to the worship music and praying for a word that would bless the members of Majestic Life Church. My car was calm and peaceful, and I was thanking God for what He was going to do in the worship service when my cell phone rang.

My church administrator, who happens to be my twin sister, René, was on the line. She seemed confused and hesitant as she told me of a strange e-mail I had received. It was from a woman in California who claimed she was my ex-husband's girlfriend. In her message she said Zach had passed away. I thought the e-mail had to be a prank from a lunatic, but I asked René to call the number the woman left and see what in the world she was talking about.

As I pulled into the church parking lot, I was nervous and not ready to hear what my sister had found out. When I walked into my sister's office, she told me the woman seemed legitimate, so I called her. The woman was very pleasant, and said Zach spoke highly of me. She then proceeded to tell me that she had not heard from Zach for several days. She was

185

used to him calling her regularly to check on her, but he hadn't. She said she called him repeatedly but received no response until a police officer answered his phone and told her he was deceased in New York.

I thought this had to be a sick joke. I called the church Zach pastored to see if he was there. When I was told that he had not arrived yet and no one had heard from him since Thursday, I knew something was terribly wrong.

I couldn't breathe. I couldn't think straight. This couldn't be happening. I left church immediately to be with our children, who were at home with my parents preparing for church. When I walked in, the children met me with a fountain of questions: Why was I back at home? Why weren't they going to church? My heart pounded in my chest as I looked into their innocent eyes. What should I say? How should I say it? What if this is a prank? What if it is true?

My children stared at me as I was gathering my thoughts and asking God for wisdom. When I opened my mouth, it felt as though I was speaking in slow motion. I told them, "There is a rumor that your dad may have passed away. I don't want you to hear it from anyone else if it is true, especially not through Facebook."

The children were in shock. Tears started streaming down their faces, and I could feel their bodies shaking as I held them tightly, trying to bring some comfort.

I called the morgue in New York, and they confirmed there was a body there with identification belonging to my ex-husband. He had been found dead in a New York hotel room. The cause was still unknown.

I spoke to leaders at my ex's church and suggested that they tell the members what I told my children. I didn't think the church should hear the news from anyone else. Unfortunately the rumors of Zach's death spread quickly. Church members began receiving text messages from friends and family members all over the United States. Questions were swirling, and a spirit of confusion began to manifest.

That afternoon I flew to New York with two staff members from Zach's church to identify his body. Zach's mother was meeting us there. The flight seemed to take forever. I sat on the plane, praying there was some type of mix-up. I hoped the man lying in the morgue was not Zach.

I wasn't ready to lose him. I wanted to see the man who made me laugh; the man who was a tremendous visionary; the man who was a master marketer; the man who was a little spoiled, a little selfish, a little high-strung, and a lot bossy; the man I affectionately called George Jefferson, after the ambitious, opinionated character in *The Jeffersons*. My mind could not comprehend the magnitude of what was happening.

I had been married to this man for fifteen years, and I loved the person I once knew—before the money and the fame. I loved the man who was sold out to God and believed in holiness and integrity. Even after his infidelity was brought to light and we went through the long, painful process of ending our marriage, I always thought one day the man I knew would return. I am not saying he no longer had integrity, but he had changed. I wanted to see him the way I once knew him. I wanted my friend back.

That hope died the next day at the morgue. As I stared at Zach's lifeless body, I began to weep. I wept for the man I had married. I wept for the father of my children. I wept for what could have been but now could never be.

My sadness was soon mixed with anger. I couldn't help but think that if he hadn't been allowed to keep ministering without being healed, if he hadn't been allowed to travel without accountability, if he had humbled himself and taken more time away from the pulpit after his infidelity was exposed, I might not be standing here.

A brief peace fell over me when I thought of how God orchestrated our trip to Puerto Rico a few days before he passed. We had not taken a family vacation in more than three years. Thank God for his mother and her persistence. She pushed him to plan the trip. I was surprised when he called and asked me to come to Puerto Rico with him, the kids, and his mom. But I thought the vacation would be good for all of us.

He said he couldn't stay for the entire week but only two days because he had work to do and could not rearrange his schedule. On his last morning in Puerto Rico, he came into my hotel room to say good-bye.

We spoke briefly about how much the kids were enjoying us all being together. We also discussed how we felt about each other.

He said he told the attendees at his recent relationship conference I was a good woman, that he could have fought for his family, and that he did not listen to the right people after his fall. He also told me he wished the conference had been recorded so I could hear what he said for myself. He then began to name people who would vouch for what he was saying.

I knew in that moment that he still loved me, but I also knew he had moved on with his life. There was no denying that our history would forever connect us, but our relationship was different now. I felt at ease with him, and I could tell he felt comfortable with me as well. We were behaving as old friends who knew each other inside and out. Yet there was still something unfamiliar about the man standing before me. He now had experiences I knew nothing about. There was a part of him that I didn't know and would never be privy to.

I told him he should stay with us in Puerto Rico because the children, especially our two daughters, were opening up to him and beginning to heal from the pain of the past four years. He said he was unable to stay; then he walked over to me and gave me a tight embrace. We had not embraced in a long time, and I could feel the sincerity of his touch. Tears filled my eyes, but I had no idea this would be the last time I would see him alive. God gave the children, his mother, and me time to spend with him before he died. What a mighty God we serve.

UNEXPECTED FINALITY

My ex-husband's death brought an unexpected finality. My four beautiful children would no longer have their father around. Zach would not see his dreams for the church we founded come to pass. He was a man of great vision who in many ways was just beginning to make the impact he dreamed of having. Like so many others, I mourned the loss of what could have been.

When life takes an unexpected turn and their hopes and dreams are dashed, some people get angry with God or even lose faith in Him. They think that because their ex remarried or their business failed or the cancer returned worse than before, God is not concerned about them.

In John 11, Lazarus's sisters, Mary and Martha, faced this kind of disappointment. Jesus arrived in Bethany four days after their brother had fallen sick and died. Mary and Martha knew that if Jesus had been there, their brother would still be alive. Why did He take so long? Perhaps you've thought the same thing. If only God had stepped in, that loved one would not have died, that house would not have been lost to foreclosure, that relationship would not have ended.

But as we discussed in chapter 2, Jesus intentionally waited to see about Lazarus. His ways are not our ways. Jesus had a purpose in His delay. He wanted to use the situation to strengthen their faith. Let's look closely at this passage in John 11 to see what we must do when circumstances unexpectedly bring our hopes and dreams to an end.

Don't hide from God

The Bible says in John 11:20, that when she heard Jesus was coming, Martha went out to meet Him, but her sister Mary stayed in the house. Mary was hurting. She could not comprehend why Jesus waited two days to come. She loved Jesus deeply and was hurt that He did not immediately return to see about her brother. She knew that if He had been there, Lazarus would not have died. To Mary, Jesus's actions were callous, and she didn't want to see Jesus or talk to Him.

Isn't that what many of us do when we don't get our way after praying, fasting, and standing in faith? Some of us take a sabbatical from church. We stop seeking God because we think there's no use. Or we lose our zeal for the things of God. Mary knew Jesus was the Messiah, the Son of God, yet she refused to go out to meet Him. Her pain caused her to hide from her Savior.

When faced with the reality that our hopes and dreams will not come to pass, we tend to put up walls so we won't be disappointed again. But the Bible commands us to run to the Lord in our darkest hour. Even when we have no clue why God didn't answer our prayers the way we had hoped, we must not blame the Lord. We must trust Him in the midst of the pain.

Take Jesus where you laid it

Jesus asked a profound question in John 11:34: "And [Jesus] said, Where have ye laid him?" (KJV). The Jews taught that a person's spirit left his body after three days, so raising a man who had been dead four days seemed impossible. But Jesus asked Mary and Martha where they laid Lazarus because He wanted to know where they put their dead, hopeless situation.

He asks the same thing of us. Where did you lay your hope that God would come through for you? Did you lay it at the office, where you drowned yourself in work? Did you bury it in ungodly relationships, wanting to feel loved and accepted? Did you lay it in church, wanting to feel spiritual though you have not had any real communion with God in months? Have you forgotten where you put it because you buried it so long ago? Where have you laid your hope that God has a good plan for you?

When hope dies, it begins to rot, and the decay will contaminate our lives and create dysfunction. Sometimes we are not even aware what is at the root of our pain and self-destructive behavior. That is why we must be still before the Lord long enough to let Him show us the source of our hurts.

I think it's interesting that Jesus asked, "Where have ye laid him?" knowing full well where Lazarus was. Jesus already knows where your hope died too. He already knows where and when your hurt began, and where and when your hurt ends. So why does Jesus ask us where we laid our dead situation? Jesus wants us to take Him to the place of our hurt and dysfunction so He can bring deliverance. As we have seen throughout this book, identifying the dysfunction in your life is only half the battle. In order for deliverance to manifest, we must get to the source. We must take the Lord to the place where we buried the pain.

Roll the stone away

When Jesus was taken to the place where Lazarus was buried, He made a surprising request. "Jesus said, Take ye away the stone" (John 11:39, KJV). Martha, being the practical one, said, "Lord, by this time he stinketh: for he hath been dead four days" (v. 39, KJV). And Jesus answered, "Said I not unto thee, that, if thou wouldest believe, thou shouldest see the glory of God?" (v. 40, KJV). Then the Bible says they took away the stone from the place where Lazarus lay, and Jesus lifted His eyes to heaven and thanked His Father.

It is not enough just to take Jesus to your pain. He requires that you roll the stone away from the place it has been buried, even if that means facing something foul. When I was a youngster playing at my grandmother's house, I would occasionally see dog droppings in the front yard. Even if I was close to it, I could not smell it because it had gotten hard after being in the yard for a few days. But as soon as someone stepped in it, the smell would permeate the air.

This is often what happens with our hearts. We can go through life without anyone, including ourselves, recognizing our pain and dysfunction. We have buried our issues so long the abnormal has become normal to us. It isn't until we obey Jesus's instructions to roll away the stone that we begin to smell the stench in our lives.

Things that have been buried for a while usually stink horribly when we dig them up, and it may seem easier to leave well enough alone. But Jesus doesn't want to leave well enough alone. He abhors Band-Aid therapy. He wants to remove the cancerous tumors growing unseen in our hearts. In order to perform this delicate surgery, Jesus requires us to expose what's eating away at our peace and joy. He insists that we unearth the pain so He can bring healing.

Walk in freedom

When the stone had been rolled away, Jesus cried out in a loud voice, "Lazarus, come forth" (John 11:43, KJV). And the Bible says the man who had been dead came forth. But he was still bound hand and foot with grave clothes, and his face was covered with a napkin. So Jesus told the people gathered around to "loose him, and let him go" (v. 44, KJV).

I love this scripture. Jesus not only raised the dead, but He also commanded everything that had Lazarus bound to release its grip. When Jesus calls you to come forth, it is a done deal. The grave has to release you, and anything resembling death or captivity must let you go. You will be loosed to walk in true freedom in Christ, and that is what you must do. Lazarus didn't walk around with strips of cloth covering him. Neither should we live in the grip of rejection, unbelief, or fear. When we have been loosed, we should walk like it.

Every chance I get I thank the Lord that my ex-husband and I were on good terms when he passed. After I took Jesus to my pain and allowed Him to heal me and set me free, I refused to wear the grave clothes of unforgiveness. I thank God we were moving forward in life, not looking back. I can only imagine the torment I would have felt if we never walked in forgiveness. Zach knew the children and I loved him before he died. And we know that he knew we loved him because forgiveness paved the way for us to spend time together.

One of the visions God has given me is to establish a Pastors Advance Center in honor of Pastor Zachery Tims, Jr. This center will help restore and rebuild pastors and other ministry leaders. These men and women of God will be able to stay at the facility for a minimum of three months to receive healing from sexual addictions, drug addictions, sexual-identity crises, anger, and burnout. Through this ministry pastors will learn how to be free in Christ, love themselves, build healthy relationships with their spouses and children, love the sheep God has given them, develop accountability teams, and truly rest in the Lord.

As Christians our calling is always to advance the kingdom of God. I believe God wants to use my journey to leave a deposit of victory and joy in your heart. When you put your trust in Him, God will give you victory over every test. He will give you joy in Him and cause you to maneuver through trials with a supernatural peace that surpasses natural understanding.

When we operate by the Spirit of the Lord, the fruit of joy will manifest strongly in our lives. We will be able to stand and boldly count it all joy when we are faced with diverse trials and temptation because we'll know that God is using them to reveal His glory and do a greater work in our lives.

NOTES

CHAPTER 1
WHEN YOUR WORLD FALLS APART

1. Library of Congress, "Family Tragedy," http://www.loc.gov/exhibits/americancolony/amcolony-family.html (accessed September 12, 2011).

2. "It Is Well With My Soul" by Horatio G. Spafford. Public domain. Image of handwritten lyrics available at Library of Congress, http://www.loc.gov/exhibits/americancolony/images/ac0008s.jpg (accessed October 14, 2011).

3. Ernest Luning, "Attorney General Directs U.S. Marshals to Protect Abortion Clinics, Providers," Colorado Independent, May 31, 2009.

4. Ibid.

5. Biblesoft's *New Exhaustive Strong's Numbers and Concordance with Expanded Greek-Hebrew Dictionary*, PC Study Bible 3, s.v. "*Be'er la-Chay Ro'iy*," OT:883.

CHAPTER 2
WHY ME?

1. *Merriam-Webster's Collegiate Dictionary*, 11th edition (Springfield, MA: Merriam-Webster, Inc.), s.v. "why."

2. Stelman Smith and Judson Cornwall, *The Exhaustive Dictionary of Bible Names* (Alachua, FL: Bridge-Logos, 1998), 75.

3. Biblesoft's *New Exhaustive Strong's Numbers and Concordance with Expanded Greek-Hebrew Dictionary*, s.v. "*shenayim*," OT:8145.

4. Ibid., s.v. "*chodesh*," OT:2318.

5. Ibid., s.v. "*dunamis*," NT:1411.

6. "Bones 'R' Us," University of Southampton, England, http://www.som.soton.ac.uk/research/dohad/groups/bone/bones.asp (accessed October 14, 2011).

7. Innes C. Cuthill, "Ultraviolet Vision in Birds," in Peter J. B. Slater, *Advances in the Study of Behavior* (Oxford, England: Academic Press), 161; as referenced in Wikipedia.com, s.v. "Visible Spectrum," http://en.wikipedia.org/wiki/Visible_spectrum (accessed November 3, 2011).

8. "I Give Myself Away" by William McDowell and Sam Hinn.

CHAPTER 3
PROCESSING THE PAIN

1. *A LifeCare Guide to Helping Others Cope With Grief* (Shelton, CT: LifeCare, Inc., 2001), 4.

2. *Merriam-Webster's Collegiate Dictionary*, s.v. "transition."

3. Dictionary.com, s.v. "process," http://dictionary.reference.com/browse/process (accessed November 2, 2011).

4. Victor Turner, "Betwixt and Between: The Liminal Period in Rites of Passage," as included in *Betwixt and Between: Patterns of Masculine and Feminine Initiation*, Louise Carus Mahdi, Steven Foster, and Meredith Little, ed. (Peru, IL: Open Court Publishing Company); Richard E. Palmer, "The Liminality of Hermes and the Meaning of Hermeneutics," MacMurray College, Jacksonville, Illinois, http://www.mac.edu/faculty/richardpalmer/liminality.html (accessed October 14, 2011).

5. Mitch Stacy and Tamara Lush, "Police: Army Officer's Wife Kills Her 2 'Mouthy' Teens," Associated Press, January 28, 2011, http://www.msnbc.msn.com/id/41319561/ns/us_news-crime_and_courts/t/police-army-officers-wife-kills-her-mouthy-teens/ (accessed September 15, 2011).

6. "Thin Line Between Love and Hate" words and music by Richard Poindexter, Robert Eugene Poindexter, and Jackie Members. Copyright © 1971 (renewed) Cotillion Music Inc. All rights reserved. Used by permission.

7. Project Creation, "Butterflies: The Miracle of Metamorphosis," http://projectcreation.org/creation_station/station_detail.php?PRKey=32 (accessed November 14, 2011); Tracy V. Wilson, "How Caterpillars Work," How Stuff Works, http://science.howstuffworks.com/environmental/life/zoology/insects-arachnids/caterpillar3.htm (accessed November 14, 2011).

CHAPTER 4
HELP! IS ANYBODY OUT THERE?

1. "You Are My Friend" by Armstead Edwards, James Ellison, and Patti LaBelle. Print license requested from Zuri Music Inc., Wynnewood, PA, copyright management.

CHAPTER 5
TAKE A LOOK INSIDE

1. *Merriam-Webster's Collegiate Dictionary*, s.v. "inside."
2. Ibid., s.v. "searched."

CHAPTER 6
FREEDOM THROUGH FORGIVENESS

1. The Mayo Clinic, "Fetal Development: The First Trimester," http://www.mayoclinic.com/health/prenatal-care/PR00112 (accessed September 20, 2011).

2. Joyce Meyer, *Battlefield of the Mind*, 2011 (New York: FaithWords, 1995), 130–131.

3. Jawn Murray interview with Towanda Braxton Carter, *Tom Joyner Morning Show*, CBS Radio, May 10, 2011, http://rnbphilly.com/audio/tjoyner/jawn-murray-talks-to-towanda-braxton-audio/?omcamp=EMC-CVNL (accessed September 20, 2011).

4. Lee Strobel and Leslie Strobel, *Surviving a Spiritual Mismatch in Marriage* (Grand Rapids, MI: Zondervan, 2002), 91.

5. Natalie Angier, "If Anger Ruins Your Day, It Can Shrink Your Life," *New York Times*, December 13, 1990, http://www.nytimes.com/1990/12/13/health/if-anger-ruins-your-day-it-can-shrink-your-life.html?pagewanted=all&src=pm (accessed October 14, 2011).

6. Elizabeth Scott, "The Benefits of Forgiveness," About.com Stress Management, October 11, 2009, http://stress.about.com/od/relationships/a/forgiveness.htm (accessed October 14, 2011).

7. Ibid.

8. As quoted by Philip Yancey in *What's So Amazing About Grace* (Grand Rapids, MI: Zondervan, 2002), 102.

9. As quoted by Pastor Mark Adams in "FIREPROOF: Forgiveness," sermon given March 22, 2009, at Redland Baptist Church, Rockville, MD, http://www.redlandbaptist.org/sermons/sermon20090322.php (accessed September 20, 2011).

10. Beth Moore, *Living Beyond Yourself* (Nasvhille, TN: Lifeway Christian Resources, 2004).

11. R. T. Kendall, *Total Forgiveness* (Lake Mary, FL: Charisma House, 2002, 2007).

CHAPTER 7
ATTITUDE DETERMINES ALTITUDE

1. George R. Dillahunty, "Vultures and Hummingbirds," sermon preached at Freedom Fellowship Church of God, Virginia Beach, VA, August 12, 2009, SermonCentral.com, http://www.sermoncentral.com/sermons/vultures-and-hummingbirds-george-dillahunty-sermon-on-action-138034.asp (accessed October 14, 2011).

2. Dictionary.com, s.v. "attitude," http://dictionary.reference.com/browse/attitude (accessed November 2, 2011).

3. Ibid.

4. Robert McKenzie, "Maintaining Our Attitude Even in the Midst of Problems," SermonCentral.com, added March 2002, http://www.sermoncentral.com/sermons/maintaining-our-attitude-even-in-the-midst-of-problems-dr-robert-mckenzie-sermon-on-christian-disciplines-44615.asp (accessed September 21, 2011).

5. Blue Letter Bible, "Dictionary and Word Search for *chazaq* (Strong's 2388)," http:// www.blueletterbible.org/lang/lexicon/lexicon.cfm?Strongs=H2388&t=KJV (accessed December 22, 2011).

6. "Praise Is What I Do" by William Murphy III, copyright © 2001 M3M Music/Lilly Mack Music, admin. EMI Music Publishing. International copyright secured. All rights reserved. Used by permission.

CHAPTER 8
STAND ON GOD'S WORD

1. Jenna Goudreau, "Nearly 60% of Parents Provide Financial Support to Adult Children," *Forbes*, May 21, 2011, http://abcnews .go.com/Business/60-parents-provide-financial-support-adult-children/ story?id=13648780 (accessed September 21, 2011).

2. The Barna Group, "New Marriage and Divorce Statistics Released," March 31, 2008, http://www.barna.org/barna-update/article/15-familykids/42-new-marriage-and-divorce-statistics -released?q=christians+divorce (accessed November 14, 2011).

3. *Merriam-Webster's Collegiate Dictionary*, s.v. "weary."

4. Biblesoft's *Adam Clarke's Commentary*, PC Study Bible 3, s.v. "cloud of witnesses, Hebrews 12:1."

5. Blue Letter Bible, "Dictionary and Word Search for *agōn* (Strong's 73)," http:// www.blueletterbible.org/lang/lexicon/lexicon .cfm?Strongs=G73&t=KJV (accessed September 21, 2011).

6. Biblesoft's *New Exhaustive Strong's Numbers and Concordance with Expanded Greek-Hebrew Dictionary*, s.v. "*agonia*," NT:74.

CHAPTER 9
PUT A PRAISE ON!

1. "When I Think of His Goodness" by author unknown.

2. *Merriam-Webster's Collegiate Dictionary*, s.v. "triumph."

3. Biblesoft's *New Exhaustive Strong's Numbers and Concordance with Expanded Greek-Hebrew Dictionary*, s.v. "*shabach*," OT:7623.

4. Ibid., s.v. "*rinnah*," OT:7440.

5. Ibid., s.v. "*halal*," OT:1984

CHAPTER 10
JOY COMES IN THE MORNING

1. *Merriam-Webster's Collegiate Dictionary*, s.v. "endure."

2. "What Is the Origin of Dew," International Organization for Dew Utilization, http://www.opur.fr/angl/phenomene_physique_ang.htm

(accessed November 3, 2011); Encyclopedia Britannica, s.v. "dew," http://www.britannica.com/EBchecked/topic/160405/dew (accessed October 14, 2011).

3. Kevin Taylor, "It's Dew Time," added March 2000, SermonCentral.com, http://www.sermoncentral.com/sermons/its-dew-time-kevin-taylor-sermon-on-gods-provisions-31373.asp (accessed October 14, 2011).

4. Biblesoft's *New Exhaustive Strong's Numbers and Concordance with Expanded Greek-Hebrew Dictionary*, s.v. "joy," "rejoicing," "happiness."

5. "Like the Dew" by Tom Bynum. Used by permission of Tom Bynum and Bynum Publishing.

CHAPTER 11
BEAUTY FOR ASHES

1. Biblesoft's *New Exhaustive Strong's Numbers and Concordance with Expanded Greek-Hebrew Dictionary*, s.v. "*krino*," NT:2919.

2. Ibid., s.v. "*epainos*," NT:1868

3. Ibid., s.v. "*bema*," NT:968

4. "Islamists Behead Christian Teen in Somalia," Compass Direct News, October 11, 2011, http://www.charismanews.com/world/32185-islamists-behead-christian-teen-in-somalia (accessed November 3, 2011).

CHAPTER 12
POWER FOR PURPOSE

1. "Nearly Half of Women Fear Life as a Bag Lady," *Washington Times*, August 23, 2006, http://www.washingtontimes.com/news/2006/aug/23/20060823-122252-7667r/?page=all (accessed October 5, 2011).

2. Ibid.

3. Caitlin Dickson, "Katie Couric's CBS Salary Exceeds Two NPR Show Budgets Combined," TheAtlanticWire.com, May 19, 2011, http://www.theatlanticwire.com/entertainment/2011/05/katie-courics-salary-was-more-yearly-budget-nprs-biggest-shows/37921/ (accessed October 6, 2011).

4. "I Don't Feel No Ways Tired" by Curtis Burrell. Used by permission of Savgos Music, Inc. and Peermusic III, Ltd. All rights reserved.

Made in the USA
Monee, IL
23 November 2019